AFRICAN AMERICAN HEALERS

✦

BLACK ✦ STARS

AFRICAN AMERICAN HEALERS

✦

CLINTON COX

JIM HASKINS, GENERAL EDITOR

John Wiley & Sons, Inc.
New York • Chichester • Weinheim • Brisbane • Singapore • Toronto

This book is printed on acid-free paper. ∞

Published by John Wiley & Sons, Inc.
Published simultaneously in Canada
Design and composition by Navta Associates, Inc.

This publication is designed to provide accurate and authoritative information in regard
to the subject matter covered. It is sold with the understanding that the publisher is
not engaged in rendering professional services. If professional advice or other expert
assistance is required, the services of a competent professional person should be sought.

Library of Congress Cataloging-in-Publication Data

Cox, Clinton.
African American Healers / Clinton Cox.
p. cm. — (Black Star biography series)
Includes bibliographical references and index.
Summary: Profiles thirty notable African Americans in the
health field, including Civil War nurse Susie King Taylor, Dr.
Charles Drew, father of the blood bank, and young pioneering surgeon
Ben Carson.
ISBN 0-471-24650-6 (alk. paper)
1. Afro-American physicians Biography Juvenile literature.
[1. Physicians. 2. Afro-Americans Biography.] I. Title.
II. Series: Black Stars (New York, N.Y.)
R695.C69 2000   99-29978
610'.92'273—dc21

Printed in the United States of America
10 9 8 7 6 5 4 3 2 1

CONTENTS

ACKNOWLEDGMENTS

I am grateful to my wife, Anita, for all of her help, and to the many librarians who were so generous with their assistance. The staff at the Schenectady County (N.Y.) Public Library was especially helpful. Most of all, however, I am grateful to the African American doctors and nurses who gave us a record of struggle and triumph to pass down to our children.

AFRICAN AMERICAN HEALERS

✦

INTRODUCTION

✦

The story of African American healers in the United States is a story as fascinating as that of any group in this country's history. These doctors, nurses, and researchers were and are determined to help relieve the suffering of others. This is their story.

Their story is also a journey: a journey from Colonial America to the present, from slave ships and fields to the most modern laboratories and operating rooms in the world. There were black healers throughout American history.

In the early years, for example, a black man named James Durham, though born into slavery in 1762, managed to study medicine. He discovered an effective method for treating diphtheria, one of the most widespread diseases of his time.

In the 1800s, black doctors ministered to escaping slaves, served in the Union army in the Civil War, and founded medical schools. One of the healers was a black teenager, Susie King Taylor. She helped nurse black Union army soldiers in the Civil War.

Entering the twentieth century, the number of black medical students grew slowly but steadily. Dr. Charles Richard Drew became a pioneer in the development of blood plasma during World War II. By the 1980s, there were black specialists and health administrators in fields ranging from heart surgery and oncology (the study and treatment of cancers) to ophthalmology (eye-related disorders) and psychiatry.

In modern times, neurosurgeon Dr. Benjamin Carson, a young man who came out of a Detroit ghetto, has become "one of the acknowledged miracle workers of modern medicine."[1]

All of these healers possessed a courage, talent, and compassion that has rarely been surpassed. "He never turned a deaf ear to a cry for help," a friend once said of the great black surgeon, Dr. Daniel Hale Williams.[2] Those words could easily apply to all of the healers we are about to meet: men and women whose dreams of helping others could not be denied.

PART ONE

✦

THE
EARLY YEARS

Dr. James
DURHAM

(1 7 6 2 – ?)

✦

James Durham of New Orleans, Louisiana, the first black doctor in the United States, hurried through the streets of Philadelphia, eager to meet Dr. Benjamin Rush. Rush, a signer of the Declaration of Independence and the foremost medical man of his day, was just as eager to meet the twenty-six-year-old African American.

Although Dr. Durham had only been fourteen years old when Dr. Rush had signed the Declaration of Independence, the younger man's reputation for healing was now well known. And Dr. Rush had an urgent problem. How could he keep more people from dying in the terrible diphtheria epidemic that was sweeping the city of Philadelphia?

✦ During an **epidemic,** a disease spreads quickly and affects many people at one time.

The epidemic of diphtheria had killed 119 people in Philadelphia in a single day. Physicians looked on helplessly as patients died from the dreaded disease. Rush had already lost his sister and three pupils. Doctor Durham, however, had developed a successful treatment for diphtheria.

Benjamin Rush wanted to learn how Durham had saved so many people. Perhaps Dr. Durham's knowledge could help him stop the diphtheria epidemic.

Like other members of the black population, Durham was struggling to make a place for himself in the new nation. He had been born in Philadelphia, but the place Durham (sometimes spelled Derham) was trying to make was unusual for anyone in those times, and especially for a black man: He was struggling for acceptance as a doctor.

Durham had been born into slavery, but he had learned to read and write. Like most doctors in this country, he had learned his profession by studying under other doctors. While still a small child, he was put to work mixing medicines by a physician who bought him from another slave owner. At age eleven, Durham was bought by yet another doctor, who taught him to perform "some of the more humble acts of attention to his patients."[1]

Finally, when he was twenty-one, the determined Durham managed to buy his freedom and begin his own medical practice in New Orleans. His fluency in French, Spanish, and English made him one of that city's most popular doctors, and he soon became one of its most distinguished ones as well.

Durham finally met Rush on that day in 1788, and gave him such good information that Rush ended up reading the young man's paper on diphtheria before the College of Physicians of Philadelphia. "I have conversed with him upon most of the acute and epidemic diseases of the country where he lives," Rush said later, "and was pleased to find him perfectly acquainted with the modern simple mode of practice in those diseases. I expected to have suggested some new medicines to him, but he suggested many more to me."[2]

Durham returned to New Orleans in 1789. There, he managed to save the lives of more yellow fever victims than most doctors of his time, losing only eleven of sixty-four patients during an epidemic that raged through New Orleans.

Only three years later, however, the city of New Orleans limited his work because he did not have a formal medical degree. He

AFRICAN KNOW-HOW

Several decades before Rush and Durham met, the most important medical discovery in Colonial America was contributed by a black man. The man's name was Onesimus, a young African held as a slave by the Puritan clergyman Cotton Mather.

During one of the periodic smallpox epidemics that swept the colonies, Onesimus told Mather ". . . Cut the Skin, and put in a drop . . . no body have Small Pox any more."[3] He then showed Mather the scar he had received.

Traditional healers in Africa had apparently used smallpox inoculations for centuries, injecting a mild case of the disease as a protection against a fatal attack.

Mather published the information he had received from Onesimus in *Some Account of What Is Said of Inoculating or Transplanting the Small Pox*, in 1721. This was almost thirty years before Edward Jenner, the Englishman who is credited with developing the smallpox vaccine, was born. Mather was greeted with ridicule by most of the leading physicians of his time when he urged them to test the method described by Onesimus.

But a doctor named Zabdiel Boylston tried it on his son and two of his slaves during an epidemic that swept Boston that same year. When it worked on them, Boylston inoculated another 241 people. Only 6 later caught smallpox. (Thomas Jefferson tested a smallpox vaccine many years later by injecting it into 200 slaves, including 80 of his own. When none of them died, whites allowed themselves to be injected.)

The method Onesimus passed on to Boylston was also used to inoculate American soldiers during the Revolutionary War, saving many of them from the ravages of smallpox.

continued to write to Dr. Rush, but today no one knows what happened to Dr. Durham after 1802. Despite his achievements, the idea that black people were incapable of understanding medicine remained widespread in the decades to come. In the face of often incredible odds, however, many African American men and women wrote their names into history as outstanding doctors, nurses, and researchers.

JAMES McCUNE
SMITH, M.D.

(1813–1865)

✦

James McCune Smith was born free in New York City to a success-ful merchant and a mother who had managed to buy her freedom. Knowing that their son would need to be well educated in order to succeed, his parents sent him to the city's African Free School. This school had been established for black children in 1786 by the New York Manumission Society.

James was so bright that when the Marquis de Lafayette visited the United States in 1824, the youth was called on to welcome the Revolutionary War hero to the school. Still, it was difficult for James to succeed. In spite of his intelligence, he was refused admittance to any American college because of the color of his skin. He finally enrolled in the University of Glasgow in Scotland, as several other aspiring black doctors would do in the coming years, and received his M.D. degree in 1837. That made him the first black American to earn a medical degree.

◆ When a doctor goes into the business of providing his services to others, he is said to have a **practice.**

For the next twenty-eight years, Smith waged war on sickness. He became the first black man to own a pharmacy in the United States. He built up a prosperous medical practice in New York City. He served on the medical staff of the city's Free Negro Orphan Asylum.

At the same time, he found time to fight for "the elevation and affranchisement of the free colored people on this, the soil which gave

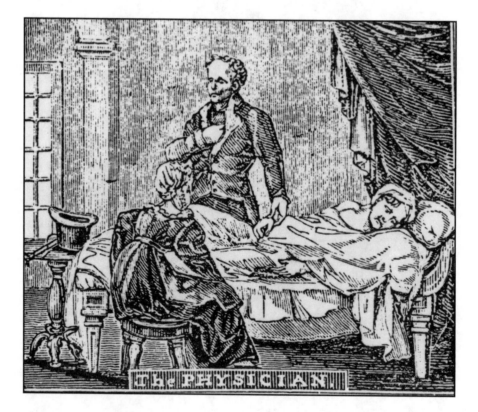

Throughout the Colonial period and for years after the signing of the Declaration of Independence, there were few African American physicians. Women doctors were almost as rare as black doctors in the nineteenth century.

them birth, and through their affranchisement, the emancipation of the slaves of the South."[1]

Called the most scholarly African American writer of his time, Smith wrote eloquent denunciations of slavery. He published his writing in the *Colored American*, a newspaper that he edited, and in the *North Star*, the crusading newspaper owned by his friend the abolitionist Frederick Douglass.

As civil war between the North and the South grew ever closer, Smith and several other African American doctors intensified their struggle against slavery. Several years after Smith's death, Frederick Douglass paid tribute to these healers.

"On all occasions, in season and out of season, there were brave and intelligent men of color all over the United States who gave me their cordial sympathy and support," Douglass wrote. "Among these,

THE COURAGE TO TELL THE TRUTH

Smith fearlessly challenged the theories that powerful people used to defend slavery and racism. When Senator John C. Calhoun of South Carolina, the country's foremost pro-slavery spokesman, argued that African Americans should be kept in slavery for their own good, Dr. Smith demolished Calhoun's argument.[2]

Calhoun argued that the recent census listed certain towns as having several mentally ill black residents. Dr. Smith calmly compared the census findings with actual population statistics and discovered that there were no black people at all in some of the towns. Dr. Smith proved that the director of the census, who was a friend of Calhoun's, had simply made up the census figures to support pro-slavery arguments.

One observer noted several months later that as a result of Smith's replies to the senator, "we have heard nothing [more] about Calhoun's learned argument."[3]

and foremost, I place the name of Doctor James McCune Smith. . . . He was never among the timid who thought me too aggressive and wished me to tone down my testimony to suit the times. A brave man himself, he knew how to esteem courage in others."[4]

The Civil War that Smith and the others prepared themselves for began in 1861 and ended in 1865, the year Smith died. He had lived long enough to see the end of slavery.

PART TWO

✦

THE
CIVIL WAR YEARS
AND
RECONSTRUCTION

MAJOR MARTIN ROBISON
DELANY

(1812–1885)

✦

Martin Robison Delany was born free in Charlestown, Virginia (now West Virginia). His father, Samuel Delany, was a slave. His mother, Pali Peace Delany, was a free black woman. They taught him to be proud of his grandfathers: an African chieftain on his father's side and an African prince on his mother's side. Both had been captured, sold to slavers, and brought to America.

Young Martin was eager to go to school. It was against the law for any black person to learn to read or write, because slave owners feared that educated black people would find a way to gain their freedom. Pali Delany, however, was determined that her children would be educated. She arranged for a northern peddler to teach Martin and his four siblings. When her white neighbors discovered that her children could read, she was threatened with imprisonment.

Mrs. Delany hurriedly moved the family to Pennsylvania. Samuel Delany eventually bought his freedom and joined his family. When Martin was nineteen, he hiked across the Allegheny Mountains to live

in Pittsburgh so he could attend night school in the basement of the African Methodist Episcopal Church.

Martin made Pittsburgh his home. In 1843, Delany married Catherine Richards, and the couple had seven children: six sons and a daughter. True to his pride in his heritage, Delany named each of the children after a black person in history. The sons were named after Toussaint L'Ouverture, Charles Lenox Remond, Alexandre Dumas, Saint Cyprian, Faustin Soulouque, and Rameses Placido, while the daughter was named Ethiopia Haile Delany.

At first, Martin worked as a journalist. He founded *The Mystery*, a weekly newspaper that fought for equal rights for black people and women. It was the first black newspaper west of the Allegheny Mountains. After *The Mystery* folded in 1847, Delany joined the abolitionist newspaper *North Star*, as co-editor with Frederick Douglass.

Delany toured Ohio, Michigan, and several eastern states to gather news and subscribers for the paper. He sent back letters every week, which Douglass published, describing the lives of the free black people he met. Once, in a village in Ohio, Delany was almost lynched by a pro-slavery mob. During those years, Delany joined the Pittsburgh Anti-Slavery Society and the Underground Railroad, where he risked his life to help fugitive slaves escape.

The *North Star* could not support two editors, however, so Delany left. Finding himself unemployed, the journalist decided to study medicine. His applications to New York and Pennsylvania medical schools were rejected, but in 1850 he was admitted to the medical school of Harvard College. Delany studied medicine for one term, but was not allowed to continue after pro-slavery students passed a resolution condemning his presence. He nevertheless managed to become a physician later by apprenticing under sympathetic white doctors in Pittsburgh.

In 1854, just three years after being banned from Harvard, Dr. Delany was praised for his service during a cholera epidemic in

Pittsburgh, and was also asked to advise white authorities about the medical needs of poor blacks and whites. He would go on to practice medicine for the next thirty-five years, combining the healing of sick bodies with an equal determination to cure the ills of slavery and injustice.

Meanwhile, the seemingly tireless Delany had organized resistance to the Fugitive Slave Act of 1850, moved briefly to Canada where he helped abolitionist John Brown contact possible recruits for an anti-slavery guerrilla army, and traveled back and forth across the country speaking against slavery.

Delany believed fervently in the achievements and hopes of African Americans. But he was becoming increasingly pessimistic about the future. He was disappointed by the failure of white aboli-tionists to protest his expulsion from Harvard. He also felt that the security of every black man, woman, and child in the United States was threatened by the Fugitive Slave Act, which made it illegal for anyone to refuse to help return a fugitive slave to captivity.

Delany decided it was probably not possible that black people would ever be accepted as equals in American society. He began to believe they would be better off in another land and should consider emigrating. With typical energy, he set out to find a way to make a new life in Africa for African Americans.

In April of 1861, the Civil War exploded between the North and the South. Dr. Delany suddenly had reason to hope for a better future for black Americans. He joined Frederick Douglass in trying to per-suade President Abraham Lincoln to enlist black men as soldiers, but Lincoln refused. Finally, in 1863, Lincoln changed his mind and gave permission for Massachusetts to raise the all-black Fifty-fourth Massachusetts Volunteer Regiment.

Dr. Delany was one of the recruiters for the regiment, along with Douglass and several other black abolitionists. Delany's son Toussaint L'Ouverture joined the regiment, as did Douglass's sons, Lewis and

A HEALER'S CRUSADE

Delany pursued several careers that earned him a reputation as a great crusader against slavery. In 1854, Dr. Delany organized the National Emigration Convention in Cleveland, Ohio, consisting of more than one hundred black men and women. In 1858, the convention chose Delany as chief commissioner of an expedition to Africa's Niger River valley. His mission was to find land for a settlement for black Americans. In Ahbeokuta, a city-state in present-day Nigeria, the *alake* (king) signed a treaty with Delany giving members of "the African race in America" the right to start a self-governing colony.

Delany returned to the United States in 1861 and wrote the *Official Report of the Niger Valley Exploring Party*. The convention failed to sign up settlers for the colony in Ahbeokuta after all. Dr. Delany, however, would become famous as the Father of Black Nationalism.

Charles. Delany himself was commissioned a major in the 104th U.S. Colored Troops in 1865, making him the first black staff officer in the United States Army. He spent most of his military career recruiting for the 104th and 105th regiments in South Carolina.

After the war, Delany remained in South Carolina where he became an assistant commissioner in the Freedmen's Bureau, which was established to help ex-slaves. He had moved his family to the campus of Wilberforce University in Xenia, Ohio, during the war. They continued to live there while he worked in South Carolina for the Freedmen's Bureau. Delany later became active in politics, running unsuccessfully in 1874 for lieutenant governor in South Carolina.

Major Delany turned his restless, inquiring mind to other pursuits. In 1879, he published *Principia of Ethnology: The Origin of Races and*

Color. The book was a blend of archaeology, anthropology, and biblical history. He also wrote a novel called *Blake*.

Delany left the South in 1880, still dreaming of returning to Africa as soon as his children were self-supporting. But that dream would never become a reality. He tried unsuccessfully to obtain a government appointment in Washington, then finally rejoined his family at Wilberforce, where he died on January 24, 1885. He was seventy-three years old.

Dr. Martin Robison Delany could boast of many accomplishments in a lifetime of striving, but perhaps his most lasting legacy to black Americans was the one he felt most strongly: unflagging pride of race and self in a land where both were under constant attack.

Douglass once said of the grandson of an African chieftain and an African prince, "I thank God for making me a man, but Delany thanks him for making him a *black* man."[1]

Agents of the Freedmen's Bureau helped settle arguments between former masters and former slaves. Between 1865 and 1869, the bureau also built forty-six hospitals in the war-torn South.

JOHN S.
ROCK, M.D.
(1825–1866)

✦

Dr. John S. Rock was typical of black doctors such as Martin Delany who combined their practice of medicine with the struggle against slavery and discrimination.

Rock was born to free parents in Salem, New Jersey, and they were able to send him to the Salem public schools. After graduating, he taught in a one-room schoolhouse and gave private lessons. But he had a bigger dream for himself.

During this same period, 1844 to 1848, the young teacher was studying medicine with two white doctors. At last he was ready to enter medical school. To his disappointment, he was turned down because of his race. He then studied dentistry under a white dentist. Finally, in 1852, Rock succeeded in getting an M.D. degree. It is not certain what school he attended, but it was probably the American Medical College in Philadelphia, which was only a few years old at the time.

Dr. Rock then moved to Massachusetts, where he was admitted to the state's medical society. He gained prominence in his new home

in the 1850s, as an abolitionist who helped fugitive slaves. Working with a vigilance committee that met in the home of black abolitionist Lewis Hayden, Dr. Rock gave his medical services to sick fugitives. He was also active in a campaign that resulted in the desegregation of Boston's public schools in 1855.

Difficulty in speaking led him to undergo an operation on his throat. The operation helped some, but Rock decided to seek further relief in France. When Secretary of State Lewis Cass ruled that black people could not receive passports because they were not considered citizens, Massachusetts granted Rock a state passport. The French recognized the passport and Rock spent eight months in France, studying the language and literature, and undergoing another throat operation.

Upon his return to the United States, he again launched into the struggle against slavery and the concept of black inferiority. Far from being inferior, Rock declared in one of his many speeches denouncing the treatment of black Americans, "black is beautiful."[1]

In an 1858 speech given to commemorate Crispus Attucks Day, celebrating the black Revolutionary War hero, Rock predicted the Civil War. He declared that "sooner or later the clashing of arms will be heard in this country and the black man's services will be needed."[2]

By the end of 1863, there were more than sixty all-black regiments in the Union army. Before the war was over, almost 190,000 men would serve in more than 140 black regiments, officially labeled United States Colored Troops (U.S.C.T.). Approximately 38,000 of them died.

Black soldiers suffered a casualty rate 35 percent greater than that of white soldiers, due in large part to a lack of medical care for the sick and wounded. White doctors usually refused to serve in black units, and black doctors were turned down when they tried to volunteer.

THE CLASHING OF ARMS

The clashing of arms came in 1861, and Dr. John Rock joined other black leaders in trying to persuade officials to accept black men in the military. Lincoln's initial refusal to allow them to enlist led Rock to declare: "I confess I do not understand how it is, that when the national life has been assailed, he has not availed himself of all the powers given him . . ."[3]

When Lincoln finally gave permission for Massachusetts to form the all-black Fifty-fourth Volunteer Regiment, an eager Rock became one of its principal recruiters.

He also helped recruit the all-black Fifty-fifth Infantry Regiment, and spoke out against the practice of paying black soldiers less than white soldiers. His voice, along with those of other black abolitionists and a few white ones, helped reverse the policy of unequal pay.

As the Civil War dragged on, Rock's struggles against legal racial discrimination finally convinced him that he needed to become a lawyer as well as a doctor. This decision resulted in his making history in 1865, when he became the first black American admitted to practice law before the U.S. Supreme Court.

Following that triumph, Rock was given a welcome on the floor of the House of Representatives. The welcome was probably the first time a black lawyer was accorded that honor. Preparing to return to Boston, however, Rock was arrested at the Washington train station for not having the pass that all black people were required to carry. But this incident was turned into a victory when Rep. James A. Garfield of Ohio (later to become the nation's twentieth president) introduced a bill that ended the pass system.

Rock's health had bothered him since his throat trouble years before, and now it deteriorated rapidly, finally ending in tuberculosis. He died in his mother's home in Boston on December 3, 1866.

Dr. John S. Rock was only forty-one years old when he died. He had worn himself out in the struggle for racial equality. "I believe in the equality of my race,"[4] he once said. And his short but fervent life was proof of that belief.

Dr. Alexander T.
AUGUSTA

(1825–1890)

✦

Alexander Augusta was a native of Norfolk, Virginia. Though born free, he had to struggle for an education. For example, he learned to read in secret because Virginia law forbade teaching any black person to read. His teacher was Daniel Payne, who later became a bishop of the African Methodist Episcopal Church.

As a young man, Augusta moved to Baltimore where he earned his living as a barber. He used his earnings to pay for tutoring in medicine. Hoping to become a doctor, Augusta moved to Philadelphia to enroll in the University of Pennsylvania's medical school. To his surprise, he was rejected. Yet all was not lost. Professor William Gibson of the medical school allowed Augusta to study medicine in his office.

Still determined to earn a medical degree, Augusta moved to California where he earned more money for his education, but again was unable to gain acceptance to a school. Like Dr. James McCune Smith and many other black doctors in the nineteenth century, he finally traveled to a foreign school: the University of Toronto's Trinity Medical College in Canada.

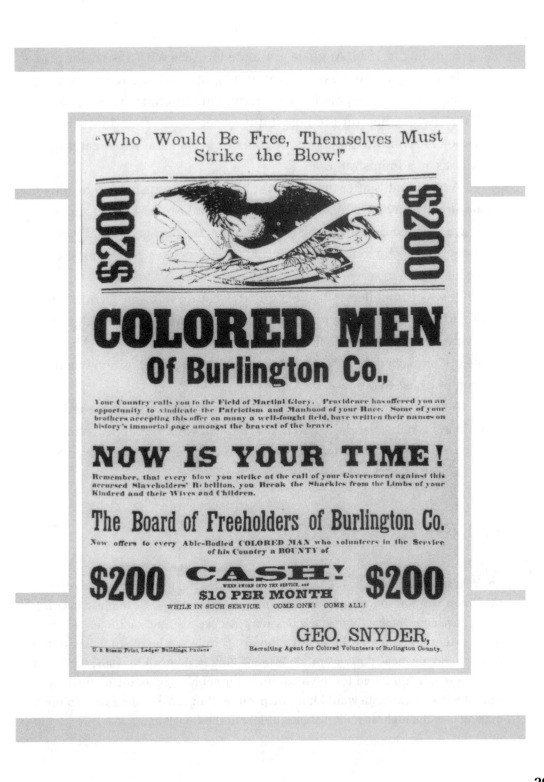

29

Enrolling in 1850, Augusta graduated in 1856 with a Bachelor of Medicine degree. He stayed in Toronto for approximately six years, conducting a private practice and heading the Toronto City Hospital. After a while, he quit the hospital in order to direct an industrial school. He continued his private practice in Canada, while gaining skills as an administrator.

A few months after the Civil War broke out, Augusta tried to join the Union army's volunteer medical service. Like other black doctors, he was turned down, but he refused to be discouraged. Finally, he appealed directly to President Lincoln, after Lincoln gave permission for black men to serve.

"I was compelled to leave my native country, . . . on account of prejudice against colour, for the purpose of obtaining a knowledge of my profession," he wrote the president on January 7, 1863, "and having accomplished that object . . . I would like to be in a position where I can be of use to my race."[1]

A month after finally being commissioned, Augusta boarded a train in his native land dressed in his uniform with the oak-leaf straps of a major. He was immediately attacked by several men enraged at

HONOR AND SACRIFICE

When the Army Medical Board turned down Dr. Augusta's request to serve in the Union army, he journeyed from Toronto to Washington, D.C., to plead his case.

"I have come near a thousand miles at a great expense and sacrifice," he wrote to President Lincoln and the medical board, "hoping to be of some use to the country and my race at this eventful period."[2] Finally, on April 14, 1863, the board found Augusta "qualified for the position of Surgeon" with a rank equivalent to that of a major. Augusta would later be promoted to brevet lieutenant colonel, making him the highest-ranking black officer in the Civil War.

the sight of a black officer. They punched him and tore off one of the straps. Augusta got off the train and went to the nearest provost guard. He was escorted back to the station by soldiers and a squad of detectives. Even with such protection, however, Augusta was attacked again. He was finally seated on the train only when his escorts drew their revolvers.

Augusta was assigned to the Seventh U.S.C.T. The Seventh would go on to fight in ten major battles, including Deep Bottom, James Island, Bermuda Hundreds, Chapin's Farm, Petersburg, and Richmond. But Doctor Augusta spent only a few months with the regiment. He was transferred after six white surgeons and assistant surgeons, who were all commissioned after Augusta, wrote President Lincoln: "Judge of our Surprise and disappointment, when upon joining our respective regiments [the letter writers were assigned to the Seventh, Ninth, and Nineteenth U.S.C.T.] we found that the *Senior Surgeon* of the command was a Negro.

". . . Such degradation, we believe to be involved, in our voluntarily continuing in the Service, as Subordinates to a colored officer. We therefore most respectfully yet earnestly, request, that this *unexpected, unusual,* and most unpleasant relationship in which we have been placed, may in *some way* be terminated."[3]

Lincoln did not respond to the letter, but Augusta was transferred to Baltimore to examine black recruits. He retained his rank as surgeon in the Seventh, however, leading to more protests from white officers who were blocked from advancement because he outranked them.

Augusta's transfer from the regiment helped him make medical history. He was appointed to run Camp Barker, the forerunner of Freedmen's Hospital in Washington, D.C., thereby becoming the first black person in the United States to direct a hospital. The hospital was necessary because thousands of escaped slaves sought refuge in the nation's capital, where they lived in overcrowded shelters rampant with disease. Out of an estimated 31,500 African Americans in Washington and its environs, almost 23,000 needed medical treatment.

Camp Barker was opened on a temporary basis to help these "freedmen" and, in 1868, Freedmen's Hospital was established to permanently "care for the national needs of Negroes who, because of the lack of facilities, were inadequately cared for in their respective states."[4]

At least 1 million black patients were treated by both black and white doctors in the more than one hundred hospitals and dispensaries set up by the Freedmen's Bureau during the Civil War, including Camp Barker. When the war ended, African American doctors and nurses were more desperately needed than ever—a need the hospitals and dispensaries of the Freedmen's Bureau had partially filled during the war.

Augusta spent several months after the war in charge of a hospital in Savannah, Georgia, where "medical gentlemen of the first eminence in that city . . . often came to the hospital to observe cases interesting to the profession, and to join with him in uncommon surgical operations."[5]

In 1868, Augusta was elected to the faculty of the newly organized medical department of Howard University to teach anatomy, becoming the first black

✦ **Anatomy** is the scientific study of the human body.

faculty member in an American medical school. Augusta also served on the staff of Freedmen's Hospital until 1877.

Despite Augusta's qualifications and accomplishments, he and other black physicians were refused admission to the Medical Society of the District of Columbia. The refusal was especially painful for him because he knew that such racial obstacles would become widespread and hinder young black doctors in the future.

Augusta left Freedmen's in 1877 to set up a private practice in

Washington. He maintained the practice until his death on December 21, 1890.

Dr. Alexander T. Augusta was buried in Arlington National Cemetery, the final resting place of so many of the nation's heroes. It was a fitting honor for the man who had been so determined to serve his country and his cause.

SUSIE KING
TAYLOR

(1848–1912)

✦

During the Civil War, countless black women served as nurses to soldiers. The nurses were paid only what they could earn by doing odd jobs around the camps. Susie King (later to become Susie King Taylor) is one of those rare African American Civil War nurses whose name has come down to us.

Born into slavery in Georgia in 1848, to Hagar Ann Reed and Raymond Baker, Susie spent the first years of her life on the Isle of Wight, just off the coast of Georgia. When she was seven, she was given permission by her owners to move to Savannah, where she lived with her grandmother. There Susie learned to read and write, in spite of the fact that such learning was illegal and carried the threat of whipping for any black child who was caught. Harsh penalties were also imposed on any adult who taught blacks to read.

But just as Dr. Martin Delany's mother had found a northern peddler to educate him, Susie King Taylor's grandmother found a neighbor who was willing to educate Susie: a free black woman who ran a secret school for black children.

"We went every day about nine o'clock, with our books wrapped in paper to prevent the police or white persons from seeing them," Susie said of her trips to the secret school with her brother. "We went in, one at a time, through the gate. . . . After school we left the same way we entered, one by one . . ."[1]

Susie also studied with a black nun named Mary Beasley and with two white youngsters who were willing to teach her. She often used her newfound knowledge to write passes in the name of her grandmother's employer, helping her grandmother to evade the curfew that applied to all black people. According to Susie, "all colored persons, free or slaves, were compelled to have a pass. . . . for at nine o'clock each night a bell was rung, and any colored persons found on the street after this hour were arrested by the watchman, and put in the guard-house until next morning . . ."[2]

Shortly after the Civil War began, Susie joined her uncle's family in escaping to St. Catherines Island, which was under Union control. She then moved to St. Simons Island and established a school for black children and adults. Many of the men on St. Simons were recruited to serve in the all-black First South Carolina Volunteers (later renamed the Thirty-third U.S. Colored Troops). The regiment was composed almost entirely of escaped slaves. It is recognized as the first African American regiment officially mustered into the Union army. (The Fifty-fourth "Glory" Regiment, officially called the Fifty-fourth Massachusetts Volunteer Regiment, was the first all-black regiment mustered in the North.)

In 1862, fourteen-year-old Susie married Sergeant Edward King, one of the new recruits from St. Simons, and journeyed with him to camp. The new Mrs. King spent most of her time teaching the soldiers in her husband's Company E to read and write "when they were off duty. Nearly all were anxious to learn. . . ."[3] She also washed their clothes, ran a school for children, and even learned how to fire a musket. But her biggest desire was "to care for the sick and afflicted comrades."[4]

She soon received an opportunity to care for many wounded soldiers. In January 1863, almost 500 members of the regiment sailed on a raid up the St. Marys River, which divides Georgia and Florida. "Braver men never lived," the regimental surgeon declared after seeing them rout a Confederate cavalry unit. "One man with two bulletholes through the large muscles of the shoulders and neck brought off from the scene of action, two miles distant, two muskets; and not a murmur escaped his lips."[5]

Whenever the wounded men returned to camp, Susie King would hurry to the regimental hospital. There she met Clara Barton, future founder of the American Red Cross. "Miss Barton was always very cordial toward me, and I honored her for her devotion and care for those men," Mrs. King said years later.[6] The two women often made the rounds of the hospital together, nursing the men and doing whatever they could to make the soldiers comfortable.

In February 1865, the First South Carolina was ordered into Charleston as Confederate soldiers set fire to the city and fled. The

HELPING THE SUFFERING

In 1863, after the famous attack of the Fifty-fourth Massachusetts on Fort Wagner, South Carolina, with its terrible loss of life, Clara Barton said she watched "the wounded, slowly crawling to me down the tide-washed beach. . . . I can see again the scarlet flow of blood as it rolled over the black limbs beneath my hands, and the great heave of the human heart before it grew still."[7]

"It seems strange how our aversion to seeing suffering is overcome in war," Susie King said of her experiences treating these and other black soldiers. "How we are able to see the most sickening sights . . . and instead of turning away, how we hurry to assist in alleviating their pain, bind up their wounds, and press the cool water to their parched lips, with feelings only of sympathy and pity."[8]

The gallant soldiers of the Fifty-fourth Massachusetts led the Union army's assault on Fort Wagner, South Carolina. They suffered huge casualties during this courageous mission, one of the most dangerous of the Civil War.

black soldiers extinguished the fires while white residents jeered them and black residents cheered them. When Major Martin Delany spoke at Zion Church, the city's largest black congregation, thousands of people packed the pews, aisles, and doorways to hear him. Men, women, and children even came to his room at night to see a black man wearing the uniform of a United States Army officer. Sick and wounded soldiers were moved into a mansion in the city, and Susie continued to nurse them until the regiment was mustered out on February 9, 1866.

The young woman who was only thirteen years old when the war began spent four years and three months nursing the men she always remembered fondly as her "comrades." She never received a penny for her work, but took joy in being able to help the suffering.

Susie and her husband moved to Savannah in early 1866, where she "opened a school at my home on South Broad Street . . . as there was not any public school for Negro children. I had twenty children at my school, and received one dollar a month for each pupil."[9] She was forced to close the school after about a year when a free school took most of her students.

Sergeant King, who was an excellent carpenter, could not get much work because of racial prejudice. He died in September 1866, leaving the pregnant Susie "to welcome a little stranger alone."[10]

In the years to come, Mrs. King supported herself and her child by doing laundry and cooking. In 1879, she married Russell L. Taylor, but almost nothing is known about her second husband. She made her home in Boston, where she received letters from some of "the comrades" and was pleased to learn that "all are doing well."[11]

In February 1898, she traveled to Shreveport, Louisiana, where her son lay seriously ill. The "little stranger" Sergeant King never saw was now an actor, in town to appear in a play called *The Lion's Bride*. Susie wanted to take him back to Boston, but he was too weak to sit up all the way, and the white railroad employees refused to sell her a sleeper ticket.

"It seemed very hard," Susie said, "when his father fought to protect the Union and our flag, and yet this boy was denied, under this same flag, a berth to carry him home to die, because he was a Negro."[12] Her son died a few weeks after her arrival, and she returned to Boston alone.

In 1902, Susie King Taylor published her autobiography, *Reminiscences of My Life in Camp: A Black Woman's Civil War Memoirs*. "I sometimes ask, 'Was the war in vain?'" she wrote, referring to the treatment of her son and of black Americans in general. "Has it brought freedom, in the full sense of the word, or has it not made our condition more hopeless?"[13]

Susie King Taylor died in 1912, just ten years after her book came out. But despite all she had been through and the pain she had experienced, she still expressed hope for a better tomorrow. "Justice we ask," she declared, "to be citizens of these United States, where so many of our people have shed their blood with their white comrades, that the stars and stripes should never be polluted."[14]

Rebecca
LEE (CRUMPLER), M.D.
(1833–?)

✦

In 1849, Elizabeth Blackwell became the first woman to graduate from an American medical school. The daughter of English immigrants who held strong abolitionist views, Blackwell was an outspoken advocate of racial equality and tried to open up the medical profession to black women.

It was another fifteen years, however, before the first black woman graduated from a medical school in the United States: thirty-year-old Rebecca Lee (Crumpler).

Lee had dreamed of becoming a doctor since childhood. The aunt who raised her was a healer in their Pennsylvania community. Though Rebecca's aunt was not formally trained, the relief she was able to bring the sick made a powerful and permanent impression on her young niece.

"I early conceived a liking for and sought every opportunity to be in a position to relieve the suffering of others," Dr. Lee remembered toward the end of her life.[1]

From 1852 to 1860, she worked as a nurse in Massachusetts. The people she nursed were so impressed by her ability that they recommended her to the Female Medical College. She was awarded the Doctoress of Medicine degree from Boston's New England Female Medical College in 1864.

Dr. Susan McKinney Steward of New York City became the third African American woman doctor in the nation. In 1896, she joined her husband, a military chaplain, in Montana. There, too, she earned a license to practice medicine.

The Civil War ended soon after she graduated from college, and the eager young doctor moved to Richmond, Virginia, to help treat thousands of the newly free African Americans. There she

BLAZING A TRAIL

In 1867, Rebecca Cole (1846–1922) became the second black woman to graduate from an American medical school, receiving her degree from the Female Medical College of Pennsylvania (now known as the Medical College of Pennsylvania). After graduation, Cole went to work as resident physician at the New York Infirmary for Indigent Women and Children. Founded in 1854 by Elizabeth Blackwell, her sister Emily, and Dr. Marie Zakrzewska, the infirmary was established because female doctors in the United States were routinely barred from practicing in hospitals, which were all controlled by males.

In 1867, Elizabeth Blackwell hired Rebecca Cole as resident physician. Cole quickly recognized the close connection between poverty and illness. Whereas many doctors believed that high mortality rates among the poor were due to ignorance, Cole blamed slumlords for creating the crowded conditions that led to sickness and death.

The twenty-one-year-old doctor was soon assigned by Blackwell to visit families in the slums, in what was the first medical social service program in the country. This position of "sanitary visitor" perfectly suited Cole, who loved teaching poor mothers how to take better care of their families despite the conditions they were forced to live in.

Cole worked in the infirmary for several years, then became superintendent of the Home for Destitute Colored Women and Children in Washington, D.C. She eventually moved to Philadelphia (her birthplace), where she opened an office, directed a residence for the homeless, and joined with fellow physician Charlotte Abby to establish a center that provided both medical and legal services to poor women and children.

Dr. Rebecca Cole died in Philadelphia on August 14, 1922, after a career of helping the poor that spanned more than fifty years.

encountered obstacles based on both race and sex, but was determined to succeed.

Druggists refused to fill her prescriptions, male doctors snubbed her, and jokes were made that the M.D. stood for "Mule Driver."[2] Dr. Lee persevered, and, in the years to come, became widely respected for her devotion to the study of diseases afflicting women and children.

After several years in Richmond, Dr. Lee moved back to Boston. She had kept personal journals throughout her career and, in 1883, published a book based on the journals: *A Book of Medical Discourses in Two Parts.* The book offered medical advice to women on how best to care for themselves and their children.

It is not known when or where this black medical pioneer died, but countless people were helped because of her desire to relieve the suffering of others.

CHARLES BURLEIGH
PURVIS, M.D.

(1842–1929)

✦

In the 1870s and 1880s, something had to be done if the masses of black people were to have any hope of receiving adequate medical treatment.

Death rates of black adults in the South were routinely twice as high as those of white adults, while the mortality rate of black children under the age of five was often three times as high as that of white children. In many southern communities, one-quarter to one-third of the former slaves had died by the mid-1870s.

Determined to do all they could to provide better treatment for their underserved people, African American doctors began to found their own hospitals, professional societies, and medical schools. From 1882 to 1900, they opened six medical schools in the South and trained approximately 1,000 doctors. Although many of these doors to education would close in the twentieth century, this was a brave beginning of a new era.

One of the men who would train black doctors, as well as one of the most remarkable physicians in the United States in the last half of

the nineteenth century, was Dr. Charles Burleigh Purvis. Purvis was one of eight children born to Harriet Forten, daughter of abolitionist, inventor, and businessman James Forten Sr., and Robert Purvis Sr., wealthy abolitionist and civil rights leader.

Charles's father was a founder of the American Anti-Slavery Society, while his mother was a founder of the Female Anti-Slavery Society. The determination of his parents to end racial injustice was passed on to Charles, who would spent his adult life as a doctor, medical educator, and hospital administrator proving that "brain development knows no race, or complexion."[1]

Charles attended Quaker schools in Bayberry, Pennsylvania, for his early education. He also learned much from the prominent anti-slavery leaders who were frequent guests in his parents' home.

When Charles was eighteen, his parents sent him to Oberlin College in Ohio, where he studied from 1860 to 1863. He then enrolled in Wooster Medical College (later renamed Western Reserve Medical School) in Cleveland. During the summer of 1864, he worked as a military nurse at Camp Barker, which Dr. Augusta had directed a few months earlier, and saw firsthand how desperately the ex-slaves needed medical care.

Purvis graduated from Wooster Medical College in 1865. His experiences at Camp Barker may have led to his next step: enlisting in the Union army as an acting assistant surgeon. Purvis served in the Union army from 1865 to 1869, spending most of his time treating sick freedmen in Washington, D.C. He was one of only six black physicians in the city.

After serving in the Union army for four years, he was appointed to the medical faculty of Howard University, joining Dr. Augusta. That made them the only black teachers of medicine in the United States. Dr. Purvis's reputation grew quickly. He was a major influence at the school for the next fifty-seven years.

THE VOLUNTEERS

Medical schools need a great deal of money to keep their doors open. During the national financial crisis of 1873, the Howard University board of trustees announced that the university medical school might have to close its doors. It could no longer pay its professors.

"While I regret the University will not be able to pay me for my services," Dr. Charles Purvis wrote Howard president Oliver O. Howard, "I feel the importance of every effort being made to carry forward the Institution and to make it a success."[2]

Charles Purvis, Alexander Augusta, and one other faculty member stayed on as volunteers. These courageous doctors went on to train more than half the African American doctors of their era. For thirty-three years, Dr. Purvis taught at Howard while receiving virtually no salary. His generous personal sacrifice saved the medical school.

Purvis was known as a harsh taskmaster. He demanded that his students and colleagues keep abreast of the latest medical developments, and was impatient with anyone who did not meet his exacting standards. As a result, Purvis was greatly respected but also feared as "a very ferocious man who barked rather than spoke."[3]

On July 2, 1881, when President James A. Garfield was shot by an assassin at the Washington train station, Purvis was the first physician to treat the mortally wounded man. That action helped lead to Purvis's appointment a few months later as surgeon in chief of Freedmen's Hospital, making him the first African American to head a civilian hospital. (Dr. Augusta had been in charge of a military hospital).

Purvis served at Freedmen's for almost twelve years, overseeing its growth in both size and importance. Under his leadership, the hospital became the teaching hospital for Howard University. It served thousands of patients a year, including a growing number from south- ern states who were denied admission to local hospitals because of their race.

Always the warrior for racial equality, Purvis joined with Dr. Alexander Augusta in 1869 to fight the American Medical Association's whites-only membership policy. It was a fight that African American doctors would not win until decades after Purvis had died. "We are all Americans, white, black, and colored . . . ," Purvis declared. "As Negroes nothing is demanded, as American citizens every enjoyment and opportunity is demanded."[4]

Purvis moved to Boston in 1905 and was admitted to the Massachusetts Medical Society. He resigned from the faculty of the Howard Medical School in 1907, but remained on its board of trustees until 1926.

Dr. Charles Burleigh Purvis died on January 30, 1929, in Los Angeles, California. He had spent sixty-five of his eighty-seven years training doctors and fighting for better medical care for African Americans.

PART THREE

INTO THE NEW CENTURY

MARY ELIZA
MAHONEY

(1845–1926)

◆

The twentieth century brought both more opportunities and more obstacles to African American doctors, nurses, and scientists. In 1890, there had been fewer than 1,000 black doctors in the United States, but by 1920, there were 3,409. The increase in doctors was matched by an increase in trained black nurses. The first African American to graduate from a nursing school in the United States was Mary Eliza Mahoney.

Mary was born in Roxbury, Massachusetts, to Charles and Mary Jane Stewart Mahoney, both originally from North Carolina. There were two other children in the family.

Young Mary and forty other women applied to the nurses training program at Boston's New England Hospital for Women and Children in 1878. Only eighteen were accepted, and only one African American, Mary. Although the hospital was headed by Dr. Marie Zakrzewska, Elizabeth Blackwell's friend and strong supporter of equal opportunity for women and African Americans, each class could accept only one black student and one Jewish student.

The training was rigorous. Only Mary and three other women were awarded diplomas in 1879. The last four months of Mahoney's training were spent on duty in private homes, where she was widely praised. The hospital paid her $3 a week to buy slippers and simple calico dresses to wear while working.

Mahoney, described as having "an unusual personality and a great deal of personal charm," was a 90-pound "bundle of energy" who thought nothing of working sixteen-hour days. Though hospitals refused to hire the dynamic young woman after graduation because of her race, she found employment in patients' homes and practiced her profession for more than forty years. (Most patients at the time were treated at home.)[1]

Within a few years of graduation, Mahoney's skills were so respected she was called on to nurse patients in North Carolina, New Jersey, and Washington, D.C. "I used to hear her praises sung everywhere around Boston and the suburbs," said one staff member of the New England Hospital.[2] And a grateful patient who became her lifelong friend declared, "I owe my life to that dear soul."[3]

In 1908, Mahoney enthusiastically supported the founding of the National Association of Colored Graduate Nurses (NACGN).

Mary Mahoney and other members of the NACGN campaigned to raise admission standards in nursing schools and for the elimination of racial barriers in the nursing profession. Like African American doctors, the nurses also tried to improve conditions within racially segregated medical facilities throughout the country. At the same time, again like the doctors, they fought to end racial segregation.

In 1911, Mahoney moved to New York to take charge of the Howard Orphan Asylum for Black Children in King's Park, Long Island. A little over a year later, she moved back to Boston, where she continued to urge other black nurses to join the NACGN.

She always fought for racial and gender equality. When women gained the right to vote in 1920, with ratification of the Nineteenth

SUPPORTING EACH OTHER

Organizations of white nurses had paid little or no attention to the problems faced by black nurses, so the latter decided to start their own organization: the first one for professional black women in the United States. More than fifty nurses founded the association during a meeting in New York City's St. Mark's Methodist Church. They quickly received the support of several doctors.

The first annual convention of the National Association of Colored Graduate Nurses was held in Boston. Nurse Mary Mahoney delivered the welcoming address. Within a few years, the organization had grown to approximately 2,000 members. The NACGN would last until 1951, three years after African American nurses were finally admitted into the formerly all-white American Nurses Association (a handful of black nurses had been accepted as ANA members in its early years, but the majority were discouraged from joining).

Amendment, the seventy-six-year-old Mary Mahoney was one of the first women in Boston to register and vote.

Even late in life, Mahoney rarely missed an annual NACGN convention, where she served as national chaplain and gave the opening prayer. The last convention she was able to attend was in Washington, D.C., in 1921, as a guest of the Freedmen's Hospital Alumnae Association. Mahoney and several other nurses were invited to the White House, where they presented a large basket of roses to President Warren G. Harding and his wife. In making the presentation, the nurses asked that the NACGN be placed on record as having a membership that was willing to serve anywhere in the world that the United States government asked them to go.

On January 4, 1926, Mary Eliza Mahoney died of cancer. Almost eighty-one years old, she left no heirs. She remained single all her life. "She enjoyed being alone at times, valued her privacy, and enjoyed her own company," remembered one of her relatives.[4]

Her grave in Woodlawn Cemetery in Everett, Massachusetts, has become a shrine for nurses, who make pilgrimages to it from all over the country. In 1976, Mahoney was named to the Nursing Hall of Fame.

Young doctor Halle Tanner Dillon Johnson was one of the few black female physicians at the turn of the century. By 1920, there were still only sixty-five black women doctors in America. Dr. Johnson, who ministered to patients in Tuskegee, Alabama, also trained nurses at Tuskegee Institute.

NATHAN FRANCIS
MOSSELL, M.D.

(1856–1946)

✦

By the end of the 1890s, African Americans throughout the country knew the names of their "Big Four" in the field of medicine: Dr. Nathan Francis Mossell, Dr. George Cleveland Hall, Dr. Austin Maurice Curtis, and Dr. Daniel Hale Williams. All four shared a common dream: providing better medical care for black patients and better training for black doctors and nurses by building their own hospitals.

Nathan Francis Mossell was born in Hamilton, Ontario, Canada, in 1856. His parents had lived in Baltimore, but had found great hardship trying to raise a family. They knew their children deserved a better life.

So one day, Nathan's parents packed up their children and most of their belongings and fled to Canada. They returned to the United States at the end of the Civil War, settling in Lockport in western New York State. Nathan and the other Mossell children were forced to attend a segregated school until his father led a successful effort to integrate the schools.

When Nathan was seventeen, he moved to Philadelphia. He and his brother Charles eventually found jobs at all-black Lincoln University in Lincoln University, Pennsylvania. In 1875, Nathan enrolled in the school, referred to at the time as the "Black Princeton" because of its demanding classes.

Nathan worked his way through Lincoln and earned a B.A. degree in 1879. He then set about trying to realize his dream of becoming a doctor. African American men and women who shared that dream were still barred from all medical schools in the South and most in the North.

Nathan applied to the University of Pennsylvania, which had the oldest medical school in the country and had never accepted a black student. He went directly to the dean of the school, Dr. James Tyson. After their conversation was over, Dr. Tyson said, "We have a greater medical school than Harvard or Yale and since they have admitted Negroes, we will, too."[1]

True acceptance, however, came much more slowly. On opening day, Nathan was told to sit behind a screen, but he refused. Instead, he sat on a bench with no other students beside him. This isolation lasted several months, but eventually he was befriended by most of the other students. There was so much applause when Mossell received his degree in 1882, graduating in the top quarter of his class, that the provost had to ask the audience to stop so the ceremony could continue.

Mossell studied in two famous British hospitals, Guy's and St. Thomas, after his graduation. Upon his return to Philadelphia, he discovered that the city's nearly thirty hospitals continued to deny admission to African American doctors and nurses. Using his own meager funds, Mossell began a drive to build a hospital managed by African Americans and open to patients of all races.

He appealed to the public and they promptly responded, especially church members and black women. Many white friends also contributed, and on October 31, 1895, Mossell opened the doors of the Frederick Douglass Memorial Hospital and Training School for Nurses in Philadelphia.

Dr. Mossell continued to play an active role at the hospital he had founded until 1944, just two years before his death at age ninety. During those last years, he often looked through his scrapbooks, which included many clippings of his nephew, Paul Robeson. Like Robeson, the famous singer and human rights fighter, Mossell was a tireless champion of racial equality. For instance, he traveled with W. E. B. Du Bois to Niagara Falls, New York, in 1905 to help organize the Niagara Movement, the forerunner of the National Association for the Advancement of Colored People (NAACP).

Mossell also was among the first to demand the hiring of black professors at his alma mater, Lincoln University, which did not hire its

WHO NEEDED BLACK HOSPITALS?

The hospital that Dr. Mossell founded, Frederick Douglass Memorial, proved its importance in many ways. For example, during the Spanish-American War in 1898, many soldiers caught typhoid fever. Memorial's doctors and nurses treated the returning soldiers. The need for the hospital continued to grow. In 1908, the hospital expanded into a building four times the size of the original. By 1912, Memorial's healers were helping 3,500 inpatients and 40,000 outpatients a year. Without Memorial, thousands of African Americans would not have had a place to be treated when they were sick. Just as important, black medical school graduates would not have had a place to train.

✦ **Inpatients** are people who receive lodging and food while admitted to the hospital for medical treatment.

✦ **Outpatients** visit hospitals or clinics regularly for medical treatment but do not stay overnight.

first black professor until 1932. And when the anti-black films *The Clansmen* and *The Birth of a Nation* came out, Dr. Mossell led hundreds of marchers down the streets of Philadelphia in protest.

Dr. Nathan Francis Mossell died in Philadelphia on October 27, 1946.

DANIEL HALE
WILLIAMS, M.D.
(1856–1931)

✦

The most famous member of the "Big Four" that also included Mossell, Hall, and Curtis, was Daniel Hale Williams, who would go down in history as the first surgeon to perform a successful heart operation.

Williams was born in Hollidaysburg, Pennsylvania, the fifth child of Daniel Williams Jr., a barber, and Sarah Price Williams, a housewife. After the death of his father and his mother's move to Rockford, Illinois, Daniel Hale Williams went to work as a barber in Janesville, Wisconsin. While there, he graduated from Haire's Classical Academy in 1878.

That same year Daniel apprenticed himself to one of Wisconsin's most distinguished physicians, Dr. Henry Palmer. Palmer had served ten years as the state's surgeon general.

The work with Palmer prepared Williams for entrance to the Chicago Medical College (now Northwestern University Medical School), where he graduated in 1883 at the top of his class.

The twenty-seven-year-old Williams then opened an office in Chicago. There it soon became known that the services of "Dr. Dan," as he quickly came to be called, were available whether patients could pay him or not.

One day in 1890, a young black woman named Emma Reynolds came to Chicago to study nursing. Because of her race, however, every nursing school in the city turned her down. Her brother, the Reverend Louis H. Rey, asked Dr. Williams if he would help her gain admission to one of the schools.

"No, I don't think I'll try to get Miss Reynolds into a training course," Williams replied. "We'll do something better. We'll start a hospital of our own and we'll train dozens and dozens of nurses!"[1]

Williams also wanted to build the hospital so black doctors would have a place to admit patients. Even Williams, an acknowledged leader in the field of surgery, was not allowed to operate in a single Chicago hospital. Instead, like black doctors throughout the land, he was forced to operate on his patients in their own homes.

Determined to make his dream a reality, Williams turned for financial help to black schools, churches, and individuals, as several other black doctors would do in their attempts to build hospitals and nursing schools.

A distant relative of abolitionist Frederick Douglass and a strong supporter of W. E. B. Du Bois, the uncompromising fighter for racial equality, Williams would spend most of his life helping black people find solutions to the racism they faced in the field of medicine.

"Dependency on the part of the Negro has always proved a detriment," he wrote in opposing educator Booker T. Washington's reliance on decisions by whites to improve the lives of African Americans.[2]

The eager doctor rallied support for his project in speech after speech to black congregations, and soon many whites were also giving money. Among those who contributed were George Pullman, designer of the Pullman sleeping car for trains; Philip Armour, head of the giant Armour & Co. meatpacking plant; and Marshall Field, owner of the largest department store in the world.

On May 4, 1891, Daniel Hale Williams's dream of a hospital that would accept patients of all races became a reality when Provident Hospital opened its doors in Chicago. Complete with an interracial staff of doctors, the hospital now provided a rare place where black doctors could serve their internships and admit their patients, and where black women could be trained in the first school for nurses of their race in the United States.

Approximately 200 women applied for admission to the first class. Among the seven accepted was Emma Reynolds, whose rejection by white nursing schools had been so instrumental in founding the hospital.

Just two years after Provident opened, an incident occurred that would bring fame to Dr. Williams.

Williams became the first person to successfully perform heart surgery by entering the heart region and suturing the pericardium. Soon, surgeons around the world were using the procedures and techniques he pioneered, and a major advance had been made toward modern heart surgery.

In 1894, one year after performing the operation, Williams joined Freedmen's Hospital as chief surgeon. He contributed greatly to the hospital's improvement by organizing seven departments, creating internships, and strengthening the nurses' training program. In one year alone, Williams performed or assisted with 533 operations. At a time when there was a high mortality rate for operations, patients in a remarkable 525 of his 533 operations lived.

Dr. Williams stayed at Freedmen's for four years. During that time, he married a Washington schoolteacher named Alice Johnson. The years to come, however, brought Williams several disappointments. Their only child died at birth in 1898. He moved back to Chicago the next year and rejoined Provident Hospital, only to be met with bick-

"Dr. Williams Performs an Astonishing Feat!"

Twenty-four-year-old James Cornish was brought to Provident Hospital with a knife wound in his chest. The wound did not appear to be deep, but Cornish's condition worsened drastically during the next several hours.

X rays, antibiotics, and blood transfusions had not yet been developed, and medical experts had repeatedly warned against opening the area around the heart.

"Any surgeon who would attempt to suture a wound of the heart," wrote one expert, "is not worthy of the serious consideration of his colleagues."[3]

✦ A **suture** is both the thread and the stitch that is used to sew up a wound.

But as Cornish slipped steadily toward death, Dr. Williams decided the only way to save his life was to operate. Surrounded by other staff members, Williams swiftly but carefully cut into the chest until he could see the pericardium, the protective sac that surrounds the heart.

There was a tear in the pericardium over an inch long that had to be repaired, and Williams began a race against time. With the beating heart constantly pushing the pericardium up and down against his fingers, Williams managed to sew the ragged wound together, then close the opening he had made. Fifty-one days after the operation, Cornish walked out of the hospital. He would live another fifty years, twelve years longer than Williams.

SEWED UP HIS HEART read one headline, while another said, DR. WILLIAMS PERFORMS AN ASTONISHING FEAT![4]

ering and resentment. In 1913, he resigned from the institution he had founded twenty-one years earlier.

During the years that followed, Dr. Williams was elected as one of the 100 charter members of the American College of Surgeons, and he helped found the first medical society for black doctors (the

National Medical Association). He also helped build forty hospitals in twenty states aimed primarily at treating African Americans.

Alice died in 1924. Two years later, Dr. Williams suffered a stroke that forced him into semiretirement at his home in Idlewild, Michigan, where he died in 1931.

Dr. Daniel Hale Williams held high standards for his doctors and nurses. He accepted only the newest methods and the best-educated medical or nursing students in his training programs.

The Power That Is within You

D r. Williams's friend and relative Frederick Douglass once gave him this valuable advice:

"The only way you can succeed is to override the obstacles in your path. By the power that is within you to do what you hope to do!"[5]

GEORGE CLEVELAND

HALL, M.D.

(1864–1930)

✦

George Cleveland Hall spent most of his medical career at Chicago's Provident Hospital. He was born in Ypsilanti, Michigan, one year before the end of the Civil War. After being educated in Ypsilanti public schools, Hall enrolled in Lincoln University and graduated with highest honors. He then went on to medical school, receiving his M.D. degree from Bennett Medical College in Chicago in 1888.

In 1894, Dr. Hall joined Provident Hospital. Before his career there ended, he would serve as an assistant in gynecology, a surgeon, the chief of staff, a member of the board of trustees, and the chairman of the medical advisory board. Hall organized the hospital's first postgraduate course for doctors and helped raise money to expand and modernize the hospital.

✦ **Gynecology** is a branch of medicine that deals with the diseases and care of the reproductive system of women.

Dr. Hall did not work just in Chicago. Branching out, he conducted surgical clinics for years in Alabama, Georgia, Kentucky, Missouri, Tennessee, and Virginia, and helped

71

establish clinics in large cities throughout the North. At a time when there were almost no opportunities for black physicians in small towns to study advanced surgical techniques, these clinics provided training. The infirmaries provided valuable medical services to poor people who were often turned away from big city hospitals or given inadequate care in segregated hospitals.

Like Mossell and so many other black doctors, Dr. Hall was also a dedicated fighter for racial equality in areas outside of medicine. He brought the National Urban League to Chicago and helped to organize the Association for the Study of Negro Life and History.

Yet Provident Hospital remained Dr. Hall's great passion. He had long dreamed of improving Provident, and finally managed to raise $3 million for a more modern facility. Though Dr. George Cleveland Hall died in 1930, his dream came true when the new building opened in 1933.

AUSTIN MAURICE
CURTIS, M.D.
(1868–1939)
✦

Austin Maurice Curtis was born in Raleigh, North Carolina, just three years after the end of the Civil War, one of nine children of Alexander and Eleanor Smith Curtis. Like Dr. George Cleveland Hall, Curtis was educated in public schools and then attended Lincoln University. He received his B.A. degree in 1888.

The same year that Curtis graduated from Lincoln, he married Namahyoka Sockume. In the years to come, they would have four children, three sons and a daughter. Curtis was accepted at Northwestern University's medical school and financed his education there by working as a Pullman car porter in the summers.

He received his M.D. degree from Northwestern in 1891, and almost immediately went to work as an intern at Provident Hospital in Chicago. His mentor was the hospital's founder and famous heart surgeon, Dr. Daniel Hale Williams. The next year, Curtis opened a private practice in Chicago,

✦ An **intern** is a medical school graduate who gains practical experience while working under supervision in a hospital.

which grew rapidly, and he also served as surgeon on Provident's visiting staff.

In 1896, as a result of pressure from black leaders in Chicago, Curtis was appointed to the surgical staff of the Cook County Hospital. It marked the first time an African American had been appointed to the surgical staff of that hospital. It was also the first such appointment in the United States to a nonsegregated hospital.

In 1898, Dr. Curtis was named surgeon in chief at Freedmen's Hospital in Washington, D.C. There he soon established a national reputation as a daring, but not reckless, surgeon. His friendly manner so endeared him to both patients and colleagues that he was affectionately referred to as "Pa Curtis."[1] Although he served as Freedmen's chief administrative officer for only four years, Curtis was to remain identified with the hospital and with Howard University's School of Medicine for the rest of his life.

He went on to serve as Freedmen's professor of surgery, head of the surgical department and chief of surgical service, and as professor of surgery at the School of Medicine from 1928 to 1938.

Known as much for his teaching as for his surgery, Curtis operated before local and state medical societies, and was the first African American to operate in many hospitals in both the North and the South. Among his most important activities were the six-week postgraduate courses he initiated, and for several years directed, for rural doctors. The courses were conducted by a faculty of surgeons.

By the time Dr. Austin Maurice Curtis died in 1939, he had received two honorary degrees from Lincoln University in recognition of his medical accomplishments: an M.A. in 1898 and a Sc.D. in 1929. But the accomplishment he took greatest pride in was the fact that his three sons had all followed in his footsteps and become doctors.

A D A H B E L L E
THOMS
(C.1870–1943)

✦

The struggle waged by Mary Mahoney to pave the way for black women in the nursing profession would have been much lonelier and less effective without the help of women like her close friend, Adah Belle Thoms.

Born in Virginia to Harry and Melvina Samuels, Adah Belle received her early education in the Richmond public schools. She was married briefly to a man named Thoms and moved to New York City in the 1890s.

After graduating from the Woman's Infirmary and School of Therapeutic Massage in 1900 (the only black woman in a class of thirty), she worked in New York City and North Carolina.

Seeking to further her medical education, Thoms enrolled in the new nursing school at the Lincoln Hospital and Home in New York City in 1903. The hospital had been founded in 1893 by a group of white women alarmed by the widespread poverty and illness among African Americans. Lincoln's nursing school quickly became one of the most outstanding of the approximately ten black nursing schools

started during the 1890s. As late as 1941, only 14 of the country's 1,200 nursing schools accepted black students.

Adah Thoms proved herself such a brilliant student that upon graduation in 1905, she was appointed the hospital's operating-room nurse and supervisor of the surgical division. A year later, she was named assistant superintendent of nurses, a position she held for the next eighteen years. Thoms also served as the hospital's acting director several times during her career, but the white managers refused to give her the appointment on a permanent basis.

Thoms was one of the pioneers in the then new field of public health nursing. She developed postgraduate courses for registered nurses and a course in public health nursing. Her greatest impact in the medical field, however, came while she served as president of the National Association of Colored Graduate Nurses (NACGN) from 1916 to 1923.

Working closely with Mary Mahoney, Thoms fought for greater employment opportunities for black nurses and to improve the quality of training offered in black nursing schools. Just as important, she also worked with community organizations and such national groups as the NAACP and the Urban League in her attempts to improve medical care.

Thoms recognized that illness among African Americans was closely tied to the poverty and racial discrimination that confined them to the worst housing and the most physically demanding jobs.

In the South, most black men labored in backbreaking jobs as sharecroppers or mill workers, or on railroads where they had to maintain tracks in all kinds of weather. Most of the women worked either as sharecroppers or in white households, in addition to taking care of their own families.

In both North and South, black people were confined to crowded and blighted housing. "Our death rate is without the slightest doubt a death rate due to poverty and discrimination," wrote African

American sociologist W. E. B. Du Bois in 1933. "As a problem of poverty, our death rate can ultimately be brought down to normal size only as our income is increased. . . . Even for those of us who are able to pay, hospital doors are today half-closed in our faces. . . ."[1]

Du Bois and others pointed out that as a result of the harshness of black people's lives and the lack of medical care, the death rates for both infants and adults were far higher than for white infants and adults. Adah Thoms helped lead the fight to close that gap.

When the United States entered World War I in the spring of 1917, Thoms fought to gain acceptance for black nurses in the American Red Cross Nursing Service, which supplied nurses to the U.S. Army Nurse Corps. Many black women tried to join, but the Red Cross turned them down because of their race. Despite the rejection of her efforts by the Red Cross and the army throughout most of the war, Thoms continued the struggle.

In 1917, she helped establish an order of African American war nurses called the Blue Circle Nurses. Recruited and paid by the Circle for Negro War Relief, the nurses went into small black communities throughout the country, explaining the importance of proper clothing, diet, and sanitation.

The nurses distinguished themselves with their warmth and professionalism. Thoms's efforts to help black nurses paid off because of her powerful belief in what they were doing.

Every nurse "who gives of her service," she wrote later, "is rewarded in terms of life's deeper satisfactions. She goes as a soldier loyal to her task, singled out by virtue of her training to help relieve the world of its greatest agonies."[2]

In 1936, ten years after the death of her close friend and fellow nursing pioneer, Mary Mahoney, Adah Belle Thoms was honored with the NACGN's first award for outstanding service. Fittingly enough, it was called the Mary Mahoney Award.

BLACK NURSES SAVE THE DAY

In the winter of 1917–18, there was a great worldwide flu epidemic. The Red Cross and Army Nurse Corps were strained to the breaking point. Half of their nurses in the 3,000-patient army hospital at Camp Sevier, South Carolina, were out sick. But Adah Thoms's nurses were standing by, ready to help.

Approximately twelve black nurses were recruited to help replace the absent nurses at Camp Sevier. Another two dozen black nurses were assigned to Camp Sherman, Ohio, and Camp Grant, Illinois. They came from several parts of the country, but the majority were recruited from Freedmen's Hospital and Provident Hospital.

"The work is very interesting," wrote nurse Clara A. Rollins, shortly after her arrival at Camp Sherman. "Our boys are in the same wards with the white soldiers. Members of our unit have been assigned to the accident and wounded from overseas ward; surgical, ear, nose and throat ward; the psychiatric; the observation and contagious wards; and medical wards of various types."[3]

JUSTINA LAURENA
FORD, M.D.
(1871–1952)
✦

During the years between World War I and World War II, the vast majority of African American doctors continued to practice in the North and the South, but some found opportunities in the West.

One who will never be forgotten by the thousands of people she helped was Dr. Justina Laurena Ford, the first black female physician in the Rocky Mountains area of the United States. "I tell folks I came to Denver in time to help them build Pike's Peak," she once told an interviewer in 1950, "and it's almost the truth."[1]

Dr. Ford was born in Knoxville, Illinois, on January 22, 1871, the seventh child in her family. Her favorite childhood game was playing doctor. "I didn't know the names of any medicines," she remembered, "so I had one standard prescription: tobacco pills."[2] She liked to prepare chickens for dinner "so I could get in there and see what the insides were like."[3]

Ford received her medical training at Chicago's Hering Medical College, where she graduated in 1899. She then spent several years as a physician at a state school in Normal, Alabama, and as resident

physician at Tuskegee Institute. She finally left Alabama to look for a place where she would meet with less prejudice.

The "tiny" doctor moved to Denver just after the turn of the century. At first, she was denied the right to practice at Denver General Hospital and turned down for membership in the medical societies. But she refused to be discouraged, declaring: "I fought like a tiger against those things."[4]

Unable to use the hospital, she followed the lead of other black doctors of the time and treated people in their homes. Soon, "the Lady Doctor," as she quickly came to be known, was treating people of all races. Besides what she called the "plain colored" and the "plain white," her patients included Mexicans, Koreans, Japanese, Greeks, and Spaniards. "Folks make an appointment," she said, "and whatever color they turn up, that's the color I take them."[5] By the end of her career, Ford estimated that she spoke at least eight languages.

Her first house calls were made by horse and buggy in all kinds of weather and at all hours of the day and night. Many of her patients lived on treacherous mountain roads, but Ford never hesitated to respond. She specialized in treating women, children, and the elderly, but she especially loved to deliver babies.

Arriving at the home for a birth, Ford's first act was to remove her coat and change her dress so the mother and child would be protected from the germs on her outer garments. Responding to people who criticized these home deliveries, she replied that the babies "were probably conceived at home, and have nowhere else to be born but at home."[6]

During Dr. Ford's career, she delivered over 7,000 babies, approximately 1,000 of them black.

After making her rounds by horse and buggy for several years, the Lady Doctor switched to a bicycle and finally to a "big limo." She never obtained a driver's license, however, and hired a relative to drive her around. During the last two decades of her practice, she

PAYING THE DOCTOR'S BILL

Most of Dr. Ford's patients were unable to pay in cash, so they paid their bills with chickens, vegetables, and other items. One patient presented Dr. Ford with a handwoven Mexican blanket, while another came up with an Oriental cloth. Perhaps most impressive of all was the grateful mother who finally managed to pay cash for a delivery that had occurred thirteen years before.

relied almost entirely on taxis for transportation. "I just pick up the phone and say my name and the cab rushes right out," she said.[7]

Many of the racial barriers she had faced during those first years as a pioneering black doctor in Denver slowly crumbled, but some remained. "This one will be of a generation that will really see opportunity," Dr. Ford said to a young interviewer, while pointing to a baby she had just delivered. "I won't see the day, you very well may, and this one certainly will. . . . When all the fears, hate, and even some death is over, we will really be brothers as God intended us to be in this land. This I believe. For this I have worked all my life."[8]

The woman who was refused the right to practice at Denver General Hospital was finally welcomed there along with her patients. And after decades of serving Colorado residents of all races and nationalities, she was at last accepted as a member of the Denver Medical Society, the American Medical Society, and the Colorado Medical Society.

The latter, as if to vindicate Ford's lifelong faith in the brotherhood of all people, passed a resolution in 1989 praising her as a "Colorado Medical Pioneer" and "outstanding figure in the development and furtherance of health care in Colorado."[9]

When the Lady Doctor was almost eighty years old and losing her sight, she still liked excitement. "Let me tell you about my hobby," she said. "I like to ride ninety miles an hour in an ambulance. That to me is good fun."[10] She had come a long way from her days of driving a horse and buggy or riding a bicycle, but the spirit of her youth was still with her.

Dr. Justina Laurena Ford treated her last patients just two weeks before her death in 1952, fifty-two years after she first began the

African American women had helped settle the West. For example, Mrs. Clara Brown, who was born a slave, became a nurse and a leading citizen in Central City, Colorado. It is said that she never refused to help anyone in need.

practice of medicine. "She had a spiritual quality about her," one of her Latina patients once said, "and it showed through her eyes."[11]

In 1987, the Dr. Justina Ford Medical Society was organized in Denver as a support group for black doctors in training. Her legacy also lives on in the home where she lived and had her office. The house, which was placed on the National Register of Historic Places in 1984, now contains the Black America West Museum and Cultural Center.

LOUIS TOMPKINS
WRIGHT, M.D.
(1891–1952)

✦

While Dr. Ford was blazing new trails as an African American medical pioneer in the West, Dr. Louis Tompkins Wright was pioneering in the East.

Louis Tompkins Wright was born in La Grange, Georgia. He was the youngest of two sons born to Dr. Ceah Ketcham and Lula Tompkins Wright. In 1895, four years after the death of Louis's father, his mother married Dr. William Fletcher Penn. A child who wanted to be a doctor when he grew up could not have wished for better role models. Dr. Ketcham was an early graduate of Meharry Medical College, and Dr. Penn was the first black graduate of Yale Medical School. Not surprisingly, Louis graduated first in his class from all-black Clark University in Atlanta, Georgia. He then applied to Harvard Medical School.

Officials at Harvard rejected his application, claiming that Clark was an "inferior" school and that Wright had not taken the required chemistry exam. But Wright was so determined not to be turned down

that he was admitted after passing an oral chemistry exam given by the world-famous biochemist, Dr. Otto Folin.

The eager youngster proved to be one of the best students at Harvard, winning a scholarship each year he was there. But during his study of obstetrics, an assistant professor told him he could not join other students in delivering babies at Boston Lying-In Hospital. Black students at Harvard Medical School were traditionally segregated from the white students during this phase of their training and not allowed to practice in the obstetrics ward.

+ **Obstetrics** is a branch of medicine that deals with women during and after pregnancy.

+ **Antibiotics** are medicines that destroy bacteria.

+ **Fractures** occur when soft tissue is torn or hard tissue such as bones are broken.

Wright told school officials he had paid the same tuition as white students and was determined to be treated the same. As a result of his determination and the support of some of his classmates, the officials backed down. Wright's action resulted in the medical school's permanently ending its policy of barring black students from the obstetrics ward.

In 1915, Wright graduated cum laude from Harvard Medical School, ranked fourth in his class and already recognized as a man with a brilliant future. That brilliance quickly showed itself. Following graduation, Wright began a two-year internship at Freedmen's Hospital, where he made the first of his many contributions to the field of medicine.

Diphtheria was a leading cause of illness at the time, especially in children under the age of six. Epidemics often swept the country, leaving its victims with damaged hearts or nervous systems, and often choking them to death with a filmy membrane that clogged the throat. Prompt diagnosis was essential to prevent damage and save lives, but medical authorities widely believed it was almost impossible to diagnose African Americans at an early stage.

The Schick test, which was used to determine the presence of diphtheria, reddened the skin of those who tested positive. White doctors routinely said the test was useless on black people because their dark color made it impossible to read the test. The result of this belief was an especially heavy toll among African Americans, who were often not diagnosed for diphtheria until it had already ravaged their bodies. The medical establishment's viewpoint incensed Wright, who declared that it had no scientific validity. Dr. Wright proved the white doctors were wrong.

A few months after his research on testing for diphtheria, Wright also introduced a new method of smallpox vaccination.

Throughout his career, Dr. Wright would combine his practice of medicine with an uncompromising battle to overcome racism both within the medical profession and in society at large. From 1935–1952, he served as chairman of the board of the NAACP. His abhorrence of injustice was born in his youth when he saw a dead black man tied to a tree and witnessed the beating of black men on chain gangs. When Wright was fifteen, a race riot raged through Atlanta, and he and his father were forced to use rifles to guard their home from the white mobs that threatened them.

THE MEDICAL RESEARCHER

Dr. Wright conducted experiments at Freedmen's Hospital that proved African Americans could be as accurately diagnosed by the Schick test as could whites. While the redness that doctors looked for could not always be seen, Wright discovered other symptoms such as swelling and a general darkening of the test area that could be seen easily in African Americans of all skin colors. Wright reported his findings in the *Journal of Infectious Diseases*, marking the first published research from a staff member of Freedmen's Hospital.

And while Wright was still at Harvard, he stayed away from school for three weeks to picket a theater showing *The Birth of a Nation*. Similar protests, such as the one led by Dr. Mossell in Philadelphia, were held outside theaters across the nation. "He felt that no one was free to vilify others," his wife said in explaining the depths of his feelings, "and that irresponsible speech that stirred violence against the Negro or any other human was not to be tolerated."[1] His great teacher at Harvard, Dr. Richard Cabot, agreed with him on his reason for missing classes. "I think that is more important," said Dr. Cabot, after Wright explained what he had been doing. "You were absolutely right."[2]

Dr. Wright was determined to fight injustice wherever he found it, including in the place where he would spend thirty years of his life and do his greatest medical work: Harlem Hospital in New York City. Harlem was a prosperous white community when Wright was admitted to practice there in 1919, making him the first black physician ever to work in a municipal hospital in New York City.

Four white doctors walked out in protest, but Wright stayed and went on to become director of the hospital's department of surgery and president of the medical board.

Dr. Wright successfully fought attempts to build a segregated Negro Veterans Administration hospital in New York and a separate municipal hospital for the growing black population of Harlem. He believed that hospitals segregated along racial lines gave inferior care. Even worse, he believed, confining African Americans to separate hospitals created a feeling of inferiority that caused "the spirit to rot and decay."[3]

"A segregated hospital makes the white person feel superior and the black person feel inferior," he wrote. ". . . What the Negro physician needs is equal opportunity for training and practice—no more, no less. Sick Negroes require exactly the same care as do other sick people. . . ."[4] Wright worked to make Harlem Hospital an example of excellence that benefited everyone who came there, regardless of color.

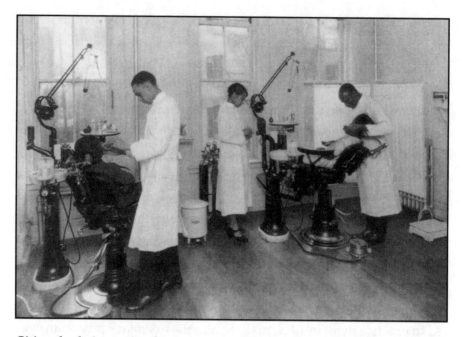

Cities, slowly improving for Americans, offered a sharp contrast to the terrible health care found in the countryside or in small towns. In 1938, this clinic served African Americans in New York City.

Wright's talent for medical research brought him an international reputation in several fields, and he loved to encourage younger colleagues to join in his work. A team he headed was the first in the world to test the antibiotic Aureomycin on human beings, and he also conducted research with the antibiotic Terramycin. Wright insisted that other members share credit as joint authors of the eighty-nine research papers he largely wrote.

He was so highly skilled in the treatment of skull fractures that he was asked to write a chapter on them in the monumental work *The Treatment of Fractures*. This marked the first contribution by an African American to such an authoritative medical publication.

Dr. Wright also invented several surgical devices, including a special plate used in repairing fractures of the knee, a splint used for cervical fractures, and a neck brace that minimized the danger of spinal cord damage when moving patients with neck injuries.

In 1948, he established the Harlem Hospital Cancer Research Foundation, the first cancer research center in an African American community, securing money for its support from private sources and the U.S. Public Health Service. Wright performed his own research and wrote fifteen papers on cancer.

In 1952, near the end of his career, he was elected a fellow of the International College of Surgeons at a ceremony attended by Mrs. Eleanor Roosevelt, United Nations Undersecretary and Nobel Peace Prize winner Ralph Bunche, and George Packer Berry, Dean of the Harvard Medical School.

His accomplishments were equal to those of any of his fellow physicians and greater than most, yet he always remained angry at a medical establishment that stood in the way of providing adequate treatment to all who needed it. His memory lives on in the Louis T. Wright Library of Harlem Hospital and at a public school named for him.

In addition, his two daughters followed him into the medical profession: Dr. Jane Cooke Wright and Dr. Barbara Penn Wright. It is a legacy he would have been proud of.

Dr. Jane Cooke Wright was the third generation of physicians in her family. She joined her father in his pioneering research. After his death, she continued her work as a professor of surgery and cancer researcher.

WILLIAM AUGUSTUS
HINTON, M.D.

(1883–1959)

◆

By the 1940s, new medical centers and research institutes sprang up around the country, making all the black hospitals that had been built before obsolete. Lacking the necessary money for new buildings and equipment, the majority of black hospitals were forced to close their doors. Where would black doctors get specialized training and information about new treatments now? For African American doctors "the opportunities are very meager indeed . . . On the whole they [black doctors] are not welcome nor desired in most postgraduate schools. This is especially true as far as clinical courses are concerned,"[1] said Dr. Louis Wright.

But the situation improved as African American doctors and researchers found ways to make significant contributions to the new medical knowledge.

By 1948, for instance, thirty graduates of Meharry Medical College in Nashville had won advanced fellowships at leading eastern and midwestern universities. Among the fields they studied were bacteriology, neurology, surgery, anatomy, pediatrics, psychology, and psychiatry.

- **Bacteriology** is the scientific study of bacteria.
- **Neurology** is the scientific study of the nervous system.
- **Pediatrics** is the branch of medicine that deals with the development, care, and diseases of children.
- **Psychology** is the scientific study of the mind and behavior.
- **Psychiatry** is a branch of medicine that deals with mental and emotional health.
- **Immunology** is the scientific study of the way the body protects itself against diseases.

Some of the most outstanding scientists and surgeons in the field of medicine in the 1940s were African Americans, including Dr. William Augustus Hinton. His work, including research and teaching, did much to improve the lives of countless people around the world.

Dr. Hinton was a native of Chicago, the son of Augustus and Marie Clark Hinton. He graduated from Harvard College in 1905 and wanted to go to medical school, but lacked the money. For the next four years, Hinton taught in Nashville, Tennessee, and Langston, Oklahoma, while studying bacteriology and physiology at the University of Chicago during the summers.

In 1909, he was finally able to enter Harvard Medical College. He graduated with honors in 1912. Unable to obtain an internship in any Boston hospital because of his race, he began the career that would lead to an international reputation in the field of medical research.

"But for Hinton's courage, determination, and perseverance, his contributions to humanity might have been lost," declared Dr. Richard C. Cabot, the teacher who had also befriended Louis Wright.[2] Within three years of Hinton's graduation, he was appointed chief of the Wassermann Laboratory, the official lab of the Massachusetts State Department of Public Health. He was also named director of the laboratory department at the Boston Dispensary.

While teaching in Oklahoma, Hinton met and married Ada Hawes. Now the young couple looked for a house as close to the laboratories as possible, so he could spend long hours doing the work he loved so much. "We had no money," he recalled years later about their search for an affordable home, "but we bought something which we could swing. We'd do so much [work on it] each year, then our money would give out and we'd wait another year to do something else."[3]

Every day saw him at work on the problems he was determined to solve: how to develop a more accurate test for diagnosing syphilis and an easier, more effective way of treating it. Syphilis was one of the most widespread and devastating diseases in this country in the first half of the twentieth century, especially among the poor. It brought horrible suffering to its victims if not treated early. The disease attacked every part of the body, including the bones and nervous system, and often left people paralyzed and insane before it killed them. The longer the disease progressed without being diagnosed, the more dangerous, painful, and ineffective the treatment was.

The most common tests for syphilis, including the widely used Wassermann test, were expensive and often resulted in false diagnoses of the disease. A more accurate and early diagnosis was needed, and Hinton set out to find it. Within two years of graduating from medical school, he published the first of his many scientific papers on the action of syphilis in the bloodstream.

By working incredibly long hours during the next twelve years, Hinton managed to develop a test so sensitive it sharply reduced the number of false diagnoses.

Hinton shunned publicity, in part because he was naturally modest, but also because he was afraid his accomplishments would not be accepted if it was widely known that he was an African American. Some southern states, in fact, did resist using the Hinton test when they learned it had been developed by a black man.

Dr. Hinton loved teaching as much as he loved laboratory work, and he taught at Harvard for twenty-seven years. Starting as an instructor in bacteriology, Hinton went on to teach immunology, preventive medicine, and hygiene. His lectures were described as "vivid," with "a flair for rolling rhetoric that often left students applauding."[4]

THE DISCOVERER

D r. Hinton invented the Hinton test for syphilis. This test, which became known around the world, helped alleviate immeasurable suffering and saved countless lives during the more than twenty years that it was used. Hinton also co-developed the Davies-Hinton tests for detecting syphilis in the nervous system through the analysis of spinal fluid.

The U.S. Public Health Service evaluated all the diagnostic tests available for syphilis and said the Hinton test was the most accurate. Officials were especially pleased because the test was quick, simple, and inexpensive, and could therefore be used for mass screenings.

Dr. Hinton followed development of the tests with publication of his classic textbook on the disease, *Syphilis and Its Treatment*. The book quickly became a standard reference work in medical schools and hospitals. Hinton always considered the textbook the crowning achievement of his life.

"I had learned that race was not the determining factor," he declared, "but that it was, rather, the socioeconomic condition of the patient. Syphilis is a disease of the underprivileged."[5] Pointing out that "syphilis is a needlessly common occurrence," Hinton said his textbook was an attempt to provide a "clear, simple, relatively complete account of syphilis and its treatment for physicians, public health workers, and medical students."[6]

An automobile accident in 1940 resulted in the loss of one leg and caused him chronic pain for the rest of his life, but even that failed to dampen his spirits. Hinton "developed such compensatory skill in control of the foot pedals," recalled his friend Dr. W. Montague Cobb, "that a drive with him was a thrilling experience."[7]

In 1949, Hinton—who had previously held the rank of instructor—was appointed clinical professor of bacteriology and immunology at the medical college, thus becoming the first African American professor in Harvard University's 313-year history.

He also taught at Tufts University and Simmons College, and developed a program at the Boston Dispensary to train women as lab technicians, a position that had previously been closed to them. During a twenty-year period, the course graduated 423 students, all of whom found employment in laboratories and hospitals.

As director at Wassermann, Hinton also helped establish more than one hundred new diagnostic laboratories around the country for the detection of venereal disease. He retired from Harvard in 1950, but continued to teach without pay as professor emeritus.

"Your name," Governor Christian Herter of Massachusetts wrote when Hinton retired, "is known the world over for singular achievements which have benefited all mankind."[8] The seventy-six-year-old physician, educator, and researcher died from diabetes just one year after his beloved Ada passed away.

In his will, he left his entire savings of approximately $75,000 to set up a scholarship fund for needy graduate students at Harvard. It was, he said, a memorial to his parents who, "although born in slavery, recognized and practiced not only the highest ideals in their personal conduct, but also the true democratic principle of equal opportunity for all, without regard to racial or religious origin or to economic or political status."[9]

The same praise could have been given to their world-renowned son.

CHARLES RICHARD
DREW, M.D.
(1904–1950)

✦

Dr. Hinton was already known throughout the medical profession when a star athlete and brilliant student named Charles Richard Drew graduated from McGill University Medical School in Montreal, Canada, in 1933.

Charley, as he was called by his friends, was the oldest of five children born to Richard T. and Nora Burrell Drew in Washington, D.C. He attended public schools in Washington, then earned his B.A. degree from Amherst College in 1926. While at the college, Drew also received an All-American honorable mention as captain of the football team.

Drew then applied to Howard University's School of Medicine, but was turned down because he lacked eight hours of undergraduate work in English. He was accepted at McGill, where he went on to captain the track team, win the annual prize in neuroanatomy, be elected to the school's medical fraternity, and finish first in an academic competition in the class of 137 students.

Most important of all, however, during his studies at McGill, Drew had become intensely interested in the field that would make him

famous: the development of blood plasma. His interest in the chemical properties of blood was kindled by an instructor at McGill named Dr. John Beattie. Drew spent hours with Beattie, assisting with his research in the medical school's new blood-typing lab. Though the blood types A, B, AB, and O had been discovered years before, medical scientists were just beginning to discover the meaning of these differences.

A person with one type of blood cannot be given another type, without the risk of death, and Drew often had to rush to find the correct type while a patient lay dying from shock. Once he hurriedly donated his own blood to a man who was already on the operating table. These experiences triggered Drew's lifelong interest in the importance of blood.

Meanwhile, Drew earned both the M.D. and C.M. (Master of Surgery) degrees from McGill, then completed two years as an intern and resident at Montreal General Hospital. When he applied for a residency in surgery at the Mayo Clinic and other hospitals in the

THE CURIOUS STUDENT

As a medical student, Drew read every book on blood groupings he could find, convinced there had to be a way to collect and preserve blood for emergencies. Several scientists had already done research on the subject, especially in the Soviet Union and Spain. Cook County Hospital in Chicago had even opened a "blood bank" under the direction of Dr. Bernard Fantus, who coined the term *blood bank:* a "central depot, . . . where donors could be sent to have blood drawn and stored for future use." But even in Dr. Fantus's bank, the blood could be stored for only a few days. Drew continued to research the blood storage problem until, years later, he found the answer.

United States, however, he discovered that because of his race not a single white hospital in the country would have him on its staff.

Faced with these barriers, Dr. Drew accepted a position at Freedmen's Hospital as assistant surgeon and instructor in surgery. In 1938, however, Drew was offered a research fellowship at Columbia-Presbyterian Medical Center in New York City. The two-year fellowship was one of several given to black medical school graduates by the General Education Board, an organization that was funded by the Rockefeller Foundation.

Presbyterian Hospital had never trained a black resident before Dr. Drew arrived and did not expect to train him. Instead, he was assigned to work under the direction of Dr. John Scudder, whose team of researchers was studying blood chemistry and transfusion. Drew was excited about the research opportunity, but he was also determined to be trained as a resident in surgery.

Dr. Allen O. Whipple, who was head of the department of surgery, was considered one of the "great men" of American surgery. The personable Drew quickly cultivated his friendship and was soon receiving an unofficial but first-rate surgical education from Whipple. "He persuaded Whipple to train him as a resident," said one of Drew's colleagues, "to let him come on the wards and make the rounds. It was a bootleg residency—a backdoor thing. He was so irrepressible they just allowed it."[1]

During a trip to an annual black medical conference at Tuskegee, Drew met and proposed to a young teacher named Lenore Robbins. After returning to New York City, he wrote her for the first time and said, "Mistress medicine met her match and went down without a fight. . . . I knew clearly just how badly I needed . . . someone to work for, rather than just a goal to aim at, someone to dream with . . ."[2]

Five months later, the two married. Lenore moved to New York City, where they shared a $100-a-month Harlem apartment with another couple, and Drew continued his research under Scudder.

Working eighteen-hour days, he set himself the task of discovering how blood could be preserved indefinitely for use in transfusions.

The problem with blood storage lay in the red blood cells: they broke down rapidly, releasing deadly potassium and making the blood unusable after twenty-four hours. Drew and his staff studied and experimented with blood that was one day old, seven days old, and several weeks old. They then used the blood to perform tests on animals.

Their experiments showed that refrigeration slowed the breakdown of red blood cells but did not stop it. Drew's research resulted in a blood bank at Presbyterian, however, that stored blood in special containers in huge refrigerators. The containers kept the heavy red cells separate from the liquid part of the blood, the plasma. The blood could be stored for as long as two weeks, though the cautious Drew insisted it be discarded after seven days.

The blood bank, which started as a four-month experiment, was such a success it became a permanent feature of the hospital. In the first year alone, patients were provided with 1,800 transfusions.

One day, Drew picked up a bottle of blood that was about to be thrown away. It looked the same as all the others he had discarded: a dark red substance on the bottom that contained the red and white blood cells, and a straw-colored liquid that filled the rest of the container.

The yellowish liquid was plasma, and Drew suddenly wondered if it could safely be used by itself in transfusions and achieve the same results as whole blood. After all, he reasoned, plasma contained everything that whole blood contained except the blood cells, and it was the red blood cells that caused all the trouble.

The excited young doctor now went to work with Dr. Scudder and others, examining plasma in detail. They successfully gave transfusions using plasma alone, saving valuable time in helping patients because the plasma did not have to be typed (since it did not have blood cells, which are what give blood its different types).

They found that plasma alone was of great benefit to patients suffering from severe burns or shock. They also discovered that dried plasma could be stored more easily and for longer periods of time than liquid plasma, and did not have to be refrigerated.

Other scientists were also working on the development of plasma and their contributions were valuable, but Drew was probably the most eager pioneer in the field. Scudder called him "naturally great" and said he had a "keen intelligence coupled with a retentive memory in a disciplined body, governed by a biological clock of untold energy . . . one of the great clinical scientists of the first half of the twentieth century."[3]

Drew summarized his findings in a thesis titled "Banked Blood," a mass of scientific data that earned him the Med.D.Sc. (Doctor of Medical Science) degree from Columbia University and the titles "blood plasma pioneer" and "father of the blood bank."[4]

Drew then returned to Howard University to resume his teaching career, but events thousands of miles away soon forced him to leave again. World War II was raging in Europe, with the British suffering heavy losses. They had been forced to evacuate over 330,000 men from Dunkirk, France, during just five days in the late spring of 1940, with fierce German fire inflicting thousands of casualties. Britain itself was under constant attack from German bombers, with soldiers and civilians alike being wounded and killed.

There was a desperate need for blood, and Drew soon received a cablegram at Howard from his old teacher at McGill, Dr. Beattie. Beattie had been named director of shock and transfusion services for the Royal Air Force in London, and he urgently needed Drew's help.

"Could you secure five thousand ampoules of dried plasma for transfusion work immediately and follow this by equal quantity in three to four weeks," Beattie asked. "Contents of each ampoule should represent about one pint whole plasma." That was a tremendous amount of plasma, and Drew cabled back: "There are not five thousand ampoules of dried plasma in the world but assistance will be forthcoming."[5]

He then set to work directing the preparation of 5,000 units of plasma in a commercial laboratory, establishing techniques that are largely unchanged today. One month later, the 5,000 units were flown to England. Drew was named medical supervisor of the Blood for Britain Program, and the techniques he developed saved thousands of lives in Europe.

In 1941, Drew was named medical director of the National Blood Bank Program, which was established to supply blood to the U.S. military throughout the world. It was run by the American Red Cross and the Blood Transfusion Association.

The U.S. armed forces ordered that blood from African Americans be segregated from the blood of whites, and be used only on African Americans. The American Red Cross agreed, and stored black blood and white blood separately. Even Drew's donated blood was segregated from the blood of white donors. Drew was outraged. "My opinion is not important," he said in protesting this practice. "The fact is that test by race does not stand up in the laboratory."[6]

Drew left the program shortly afterward and returned to Howard. He was never offered another position in the national blood program, but the techniques and procedures he established marked the birth of the worldwide blood donor system that exists today.

Although Drew's international reputation is based on his pioneering contributions to the development of blood plasma, he made an equally great contribution with his teaching. Drew knew that in the world of American medicine, with its limited number of internships and residencies for African American doctors, the population they served was desperately short of surgeons. Working his usual long days, month in and month out, he did much to lessen that shortage.

"The boys whom we are now helping to train," he declared in 1947, "I believe, in time will constitute my greatest contribution to medicine."[7] From 1941 to 1950—while serving as director of surgery at Howard's expanding medical school—Drew taught eight black surgeons who went on to receive certification papers from the American Board of Surgery (these eight constituted half the black surgeons who were certified during that period).

Another fourteen men at Howard who eventually earned their certificates studied in the surgery department while Drew was in charge. The men he trained went on to pioneer in the fields of cardiovascular surgery, gynecology, neurosurgery, and other fields.

"Charley was a believer in the vanguard," said one of his colleagues, Dr. Charles D. Watts. "If a man showed promise, he'd take him aside and urge him to consider one of the specialties that were opening. Many of these fields had only recently been developing. They were the focus of new research, of exciting new discoveries. Why shouldn't blacks be encouraged to try and enter them?"[8]

On March 31, 1950, Drew spent a full day teaching and performing operations, then attended a banquet given by the Howard student council. He had promised to help drive three other doctors, including two interns who could not afford to travel any other way, to the annual medical conference at Tuskegee.

They planned to "drive in one pop without stopping," remembered Dr. Watts. "During those times it was not easy to find places for black people [to spend the night]."[9] Bone-tired, Drew went to bed for two hours, then began the journey. Just outside of Burlington, North Carolina, he apparently fell asleep at the wheel. The car overturned and Drew was half thrown out. None of the other men were hurt, but Drew never regained consciousness.

It was widely believed among black Americans in the years that followed that Drew, the father of blood plasma, bled to death because he was refused admittance to a white hospital. Such a fate was common in the South, where many critically ill black people were turned away from white hospitals. But the white doctors in the emergency room at Alamance General Hospital, where Drew was taken, knew who he was and worked heroically to save him. They even gave him plasma because there was not enough time to cross-match him for whole blood.

His injuries were simply too massive for the doctors to overcome. "Charley was a man who was always in a hurry," his wife remembered after his death. "There was just never enough time."[10] And yet there was time enough for him to help any young doctor who asked for his knowledge and advice. There was time enough for him "to talk to the poorest, most ragged of our patients like he was talking to his mother,"[11] said one of his Howard colleagues, Dr. Burke Syphax.

And there was time enough for Dr. Charles Richard Drew to help lay the foundations of a new field of science that is still offering exciting possibilities for the future health of all people.

PERCY LAVON
JULIAN, Ph.D.
(1899–1975)

✦

D r. Percy Lavon Julian, an African American chemist, helped bring relief to millions of people suffering from glaucoma, arthritis, and other illnesses.

Julian was a native of Montgomery, Alabama, one of six children born to James and Elizabeth Adams Julian. All of the children went to universities and earned graduate degrees. Julian's father was a railway clerk and his mother was a schoolteacher. His paternal grandfather was an ex-slave who had had two fingers cut off his right hand as punishment for learning to write.

Julian attended DePauw University in Greencastle, Indiana, where he lived in the attic of a fraternity house and worked his way through college by waiting on tables in the fraternity house, tending furnaces, and playing in a jazz band. He adopted some of his chemistry teachers at DePauw as role models, but all of them refused to give him a fellowship to continue his studies after graduation. He was not welcomed at the university because he was black.

110

Nevertheless, he received his B.S. degree in chemistry in 1920, graduating as class valedictorian and a member of Phi Beta Kappa. Denied work in the field he loved, he taught chemistry at Fisk University in Nashville, Tennessee, for the next two years after his graduation.

In 1922, he was given the Austin Fellowship in chemistry at Harvard University, where he earned his M.S. in chemistry in 1923. Despite his high grades, however, he was denied a teaching assistantship at Harvard out of fear that white southern students would object to being taught by a black man. During the next few years, Julian combined continued studies with teaching at the West Virginia School for Negroes (now West Virginia State College) and Howard University.

By this time, Julian had become interested in the research of chemist Ernst Spath at the University of Vienna. Spath had developed methods for producing drugs artificially. Finally, in 1929, Julian was awarded a fellowship to go to Vienna and study with Spath. When Julian arrived in Vienna, Spath welcomed him into his own household and treated him like a son.

The two men worked together to find ways to synthesize (produce artificially) various drugs. Julian became especially interested in the soybean, which German scientists were using to manufacture several drugs, including one used in the treatment of glaucoma: physostigmine.

In glaucoma, pressure slowly builds up inside the eyeball, eventually destroying the retina and causing blindness. Physostigmine reduces that pressure, thereby saving the patient's sight. Drugs produced from plants and other natural sources were effective, but the process of extracting them was slow and expensive, and they could be made only in limited quantities. Julian knew that if he could synthesize physostigmine, it would be both cheap and available in such large quantities that virtually anyone could be treated. The problem of synthesizing the drug had frustrated chemists for years, but Julian was determined to succeed.

Julian received his Ph.D. in chemistry from the University of Vienna in 1931 and returned to his teaching position at Howard. Two colleagues from Vienna came back to Howard with him, and they continued to investigate the structure of physostigmine.

In 1932, because of a disagreement with the Howard administration, Julian was forced to leave the university. He was given a position at DePauw as a research fellow and teacher of organic chemistry, and it was at DePauw that he identified the chemicals that led to the formation of physostigmine. In 1934, Julian presented his findings to the American Chemical Society, and by the early part of 1935, he had accomplished the first synthesis of physostigmine.

This success brought him to the attention of scientists throughout the world, but shortly afterward he was turned down for teaching positions at DePauw and the University of Minnesota because of his race. These rejections were especially painful for Julian because he had recently married Anna Johnson, who had a Ph.D. in sociology. The couple eventually had three children: Percy Jr., Faith, and Rhoderic.

Fortunately, Julian's success had also brought him to the attention of officials of the Glidden Company. Glidden, a Chicago paint manufacturer, appointed him chief chemist and director of research. Julian's appointment to work in a high-level job in a corporation marked a breakthrough for African American scientists in this country, and it helped remove racial barriers in other scientific fields.

His task at Glidden was to examine the potential of soybeans for industrial use, and in the years to come, Julian developed products ranging from a new technique for coating paper to a new fire-fighting substance called Aero-Foam, which put out oil and gas fires by smothering the oxygen supply. The United States Navy has used Aero-Foam, which it calls "bean soup," to save the lives of thousands of airmen and sailors.

BE ENTHUSIASTIC!

Many healers are positively driven to explore new areas of scientific research. "Every problem grows into a new problem," Dr. Julian once explained, "and every new product lays the basis for the manufacture of another new product."[1]

Dr. Julian's enthusiasm for research spread to his staff. "He was obviously a man of great energy and ability who galvanized us all," one of his assistants declared.[2]

Julian's greatest research interests remained in the field of drugs, and he developed a new technique to mass-produce two medically important sex hormones from chemicals in soybean oil: testosterone (male) and progesterone (female). Testosterone is used to treat males who are losing their vitality because of aging, and progesterone is given to pregnant women who are in danger of having a miscarriage. Both have also been used effectively in the treatment of cancer, and Julian's synthesis of them from soybeans has been called one of the outstanding achievements in organic chemistry.

But his greatest achievement was yet to come: the discovery of a way to synthesize cortisone, a drug used to treat people suffering from rheumatoid arthritis. Researchers at the Mayo Clinic had discovered that cortisone was beneficial in such cases, but the only way to obtain the drug was by extracting it from the bile of oxen.

Officials estimated that it would take the bile of 14,600 oxen to supply enough cortisone to treat just one patient effectively for one year. The cost was several hundred dollars per gram, so only the rich could afford it.

Julian perfected a way of commercially producing cortexolone from soybeans. Cortexolone, which he called Substance S, was identical to cortisone except for one missing atom of oxygen. Julian then figured out how to supply this missing atom, thereby making his Substance S the synthetic equivalent of natural cortisone. The result was a powerful, painkilling drug that could be used by millions because it cost only a few cents per gram to manufacture.

Dr. Julian continued to do basic research, trying to find more substances to help those who were in pain. Even in the last months of his life, when he was terminally ill with cancer, he directed two companies in Franklin Park, Illinois: Julian Associates and the Julian Research Institute.

In 1974, Sigma Xi, an honorary society of research scientists, awarded him the Proctor Prize for extraordinary service to science and humanity.

"I have had one goal in my life," Dr. Julian said in summing up his lifelong efforts, "that of playing some role in making life a little easier for the persons who come after me."[3] In 1990, he and agricultural scientist George Carver were elected to the National Inventors Hall of Fame. They were the first African Americans to be given this honor.

Dr. Julian was a strong financial supporter of the Reverend Martin Luther King Jr. and his Southern Christian Leadership Conference. "Of all the forms of inequality, injustice in health care is the most shocking and the most inhumane . . . ," Dr. King declared in a speech at the 1966 Convention of the Medical Committee for Human Rights, an interracial group of doctors from around the country.[4]

Like Dr. King, Dr. Percy Lavon Julian had hope for the future. A "completely new day is dawning" for black American scientists, he said not long before he died on April 19, 1975. "He is slowly arriving; he has faith in himself; and he is becoming a calm, determined scholar—eager, anxious, and definitely destined to write new chapters in the history of his discipline. Indeed he is doing so already! . . ."[5]

PART FOUR

◆

MODERN TIMES

ALVIN FRANCIS
POUSSAINT, M.D.
(B. 1934)

✦

One day when Dr. Poussaint was still in junior high school, a teacher touched his shoulder and suggested he apply to Peter Stuyvesant High School, one of New York City's special science schools. Until that day, Poussaint had not even known there were special science schools. He now refers to that teacher's touch as "a 30-second miracle."[1]

It is the kind of miracle Dr. Alvin Francis Poussaint has spent his professional life trying to bring to other people, both adults and the children he fervently believes are "our most precious possession."[2]

Dr. Poussaint, a Harlem native born to Christopher Poussaint, a printer, and Harriet Johnson Poussaint, was one of eight children: five sons and three daughters. His grandparents on his father's side were Haitian immigrants.

In 1952, Alvin graduated from Peter Stuyvesant High School, one of New York City's schools for gifted students. He enrolled in Columbia University's pre-med program, earning his B.A. degree in 1956, and receiving several graduate scholarships. Alvin chose to

enroll in Cornell University Medical College and its affiliated New York Hospital in Manhattan, where he earned his M.D. degree in 1960.

The young doctor then went on to study psychiatry at the University of Southern California at Los Angeles, becoming chief resident of its Neuropsychiatric Institute in 1964. His appointment was a tribute to the progress that had been made by African American healers in the twentieth century.

Increasing numbers of both black and white doctors had called for eliminating racial segregation and discrimination in the medical world. But there was still a long way to go. From 1946 to 1964, for example, the American government spent $2 billion to build 104 segregated hospitals and other medical facilities. In one Texas hospital built with federal funds, African American patients were given beds in hallways and aisles, even when there were empty beds in the hospital's "white" section.

Black doctors also continued to find it impossible to gain admittance to most local chapters of the American Medical Association (AMA). Without such membership they could not receive hospital staff appointments, and without the staff appointments, they could not keep up with the latest medical advances.

The 1964 Civil Rights Act, combined with lawsuits, finally forced the end of federal funding of segregated hospitals and medical schools. But many young black doctors complained that they were often confined to certain fields, especially radiology, anesthesiology, and pathology. "In radiology the patient is in the dark and can't see the doctor," explained one black physician, only half-jokingly. "In anesthesiology he's asleep. And in pathology he's dead and it doesn't make any difference."[3]

+ **Radiology** is the science of using X rays to diagnose and treat disease.

+ **Anesthesiology** is the science of bringing pain relief.

+ **Pathology** is the study of the nature of diseases.

The struggle to gain "equal justice in health care now," as Dr. W. Montague Cobb put it, and the broader civil rights struggle being waged throughout the country, suddenly coalesced during the 1960s.[4] Nowhere was this coming together more apparent than in the career of Dr. Alvin Francis Poussaint.

As the only black American in a class of eighty-six at Cornell Medical College, Poussaint had repeatedly encountered racial prejudice from both classmates and faculty. These experiences helped lead to his decision to specialize in psychiatry, concentrating on helping black patients deal with the emotional distress inflicted by racism.

Poussaint was eager to join other doctors in the civil rights movement. Sadly, doctors were often needed. When the Reverend Martin Luther King Jr. led a voter registration march in Selma, Alabama, hundreds of black men, women, and children were viciously beaten by police and state troopers. Medical care for the injured was provided by members of the National Medical Association and the Medical Committee for Human Rights.

In 1966, Bob Moses, a former high school classmate of Poussaint, asked him to become Southern Field Director of the Medical Committee. Moses was a leader of the Student Nonviolent Coordinating Committee (SNCC), a nationwide network of black students trying to end segregation in the South.

The thirty-two-year-old Poussaint hurried south and helped organize the committee's clinic in Holmes County, Mississippi, one of the focal points of SNCC's voter registration drive. Under Poussaint, the clinic not only provided medical care for the county's desperately poor black residents, but also disseminated health education to residents of other Mississippi counties. But Poussaint soon had to participate in medical activities that were much more dangerous than running the clinic.

Four years earlier, James Meredith had become the first black student to enroll in the University of Mississippi. His enrollment met with fierce white resistance, sparking riots in which two people were killed and fifty arrested. Meredith had to be escorted onto campus by U.S. marshals, and President John F. Kennedy dispatched 3,000 soldiers to keep order.

A few weeks after Poussaint arrived in Mississippi, Meredith and a small group of followers began marching to the state capital in Jackson to encourage black residents to vote. The march had barely begun when Meredith was wounded by a shotgun blast. Reverend King and other civil rights leaders vowed to resume the 220-mile march, and asked the committee to provide medical support.

Although almost literally forced to make arrangements on a moment's notice, Poussaint organized supplies and a group of volunteers who accompanied the marchers throughout their three-week trek.

One afternoon in that tumultuous summer of 1966, when a white policeman rudely addressed him as "boy," Poussaint protested mildly that he was a doctor, but the policeman continued to harass him and demanded to know his first name. Finally, realizing the potential violence he faced if he continued to argue, Poussaint gave the policeman his first name.

"No amount of self-love could have salvaged my pride or preserved my integrity . . . ," he said of the experience that day. "For the moment my manhood had been ripped from me . . . on a public street for all the local black people to witness, reminding them that no black man was as good as any white man. All of us—doctor, lawyer, postman, field hand and shoeshine boy—had been psychologically 'put in our place.'. . . What was I to do with my rage?"[5]

In the years to come, Poussaint helped people understand that there was a special kind of anger caused by racism. He added to the scientific understanding of the ways that anger hurts people's lives. As a result, he recommended that white psychiatrists be given additional training to enable them to treat all kinds of people. Too many psychiatrists, he declared, were unable to tell the difference between "deviant behavior" and "different behavior" in people of a different race from their own.[6]

Poussaint is currently senior psychiatrist at the Judge Baker Children's Center in Boston's Children's Hospital. He is also a professor of clinical psychiatry and associate dean for student affairs at Harvard Medical School, where he has taught since 1969.

HELPING KIDS AND PARENTS

Throughout his career, Dr. Poussaint has been especially concerned about African American and mixed-race children. Poussaint and fellow African American psychiatrist Dr. James Comer are co-authors of the book *Raising Black Children*. From 1984 to 1992, Poussaint served as consultant to both *The Cosby Show* and *A Different World*. The stories and characters on those shows provided many examples of healthy family life.

Dr. Poussaint believes that it is important for parents to talk to their children. "The biggest challenge for any parent is being there and being patient and being loving and being a teacher and not thinking that children are little adults."[7]

BENJAMIN SOLOMON
CARSON, M.D.

(B. 1951)

✦

In 1987, a young African American doctor named Benjamin Carson successfully performed what many have called the most complex operation in medical history: the separation of Siamese twins joined at the back of the head.

Carson, the director of pediatric surgery at Baltimore's Johns Hopkins Hospital, was born September 18, 1951, in Detroit, Michigan. His parents were Robert Solomon and Sonya Copeland Carson.

Ben and his older brother, Curtis, were raised in one of Detroit's poorest neighborhoods by their mother, who told them "you can be *anything* you want to be." After divorcing the boys' father when Ben was eight, she worked two and sometimes three jobs. But she was not discouraged. Although she had only a third grade education, she encouraged her sons to do well in school.

With the help of his mother, who limited Ben and his brother to watching just two or three television shows a week (which she chose) and made them read at least two books a week, Carson graduated from Detroit's Southwestern High School with honors.

124

"I HAD HEARD THAT THE LORD CAN CHANGE PEOPLE"

As a boy, Ben Carson did poorly in his studies. He also had a temper he once described as "near pathological." When he was fourteen years old, he tried to stab a schoolmate in the stomach, but the knife struck the other boy's belt buckle and broke.

"It was then that I realized that if I continued in that vein, I was going to kill somebody or somebody was going to kill me,"[1] he said.

Carson, a deeply religious man, knelt on the floor and prayed for help. "I had heard that the Lord can change people," he explained. "And He did. From that day on, I have not had a problem with my temper."[2]

He went on to receive a full scholarship to Yale University, where he graduated in 1973 with a B.A. degree. In 1977, he received his M.D. degree from the University of Michigan Medical School, which he had attended on grants. While attending the University of Michigan, Carson married Candy Rustin. The couple now have three sons: Murray Nedlands, Benjamin Solomon Jr., and Rhoeyce Harrington.

Carson's dream of becoming a neurosurgeon was fulfilled when he completed a five-year residency in neurosurgery at Johns Hopkins Hospital. He was the first black neurosurgical resident at Hopkins, which named him director of pediatric neurosurgery in 1984.

During the next few months, Carson performed several daring and successful operations on children other doctors believed could not be helped. In one case, the parents of a four-year-old with a cancerous tumor on his brain stem brought their son to Carson after other doctors declared his tumor inoperable. During the course of two laborious operations, Carson removed the tumor and the child recovered.

A few months later, a four-year-old girl was brought to him, suffering from as many as 120 seizures a day and paralysis on her right side. During a ten-hour operation, he removed the left hemisphere of her brain, which was diseased. Six months later, the child was free of seizures, had regained almost complete use of her right side, and could dream once again of becoming a ballerina.

But the case that would bring Carson international acclaim was still to come.

Two German infants named Patrick and Benjamin Binder had been born as Siamese twins. They had separate brains, but were joined at the back of their heads, where they shared blood vessels.

Doctors could not figure out how to separate them without sacrificing one of the children. In many operations when Siamese twins are separated at the back of the head, one of the children usually dies from heavy hemorrhaging (bleeding) or suffers severe mental damage.

Carson studied the twins' medical records and came up with a plan to save them both: stop their hearts and drain their blood supply, then restore circulation only after they were safely separated.

Such a procedure had never been tried before, but Carson was confident it would work. With Dr. Donlin Long, chairman of Hopkins's department of neurosurgery, Carson assembled a team of seventy doctors, nurses, and technicians. The team practiced the operation over and over, using life-size dolls stuck together at the back of their heads with patches of Velcro.

At 7:00 A.M. on September 5, 1987, they began the operation. It was scheduled to last twenty-two hours, with only one hour allowed to separate the twins' tangled blood vessels after their hearts were stopped and their blood drained.

At first, all went well. But as Carson probed deeper into the brains, he discovered that the vessels that carried blood from each baby's brain to his heart were much more tangled than expected. At last, twenty minutes after draining their blood, he made the final cut in the vessels. Now it was a race against time.

With only forty minutes left to rebuild the blood vessels in each twin's head and patch the places where they had been joined, Carson and his team began working on Patrick. Long and his team did the same with Benjamin.

They fashioned new veins out of heart tissue and stretched skin over the parts of the babies' heads where they had been joined. Finally, just before the time was up, they finished the operation. No longer were Patrick and Benjamin Binder Siamese twins: Now they were simply twins, thanks to a history-making operation born in the mind of Dr. Benjamin Solomon Carson.

"Nobody was born to be a failure," he told the graduating class at Southwestern High School several months later. "If you feel you're going to succeed, and you work your tail off, you will succeed!"[3]

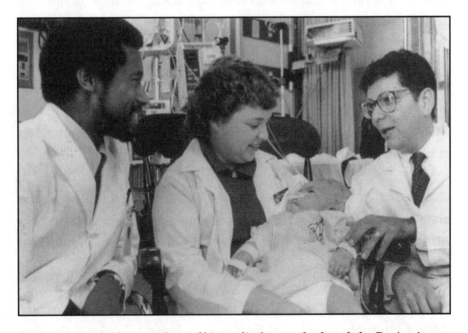

Dr. Carson and other members of his medical team check on baby Benjamin Binder after their landmark operation.

DEBORAH

PROTHROW-STITH, M.D.

(B. 1954)

✦

Dr. Deborah Prothrow-Stith sees violence as the most dangerous health threat faced by young Americans, especially those who are poor and black.

Prothrow-Stith, a native of Marshall, Texas, was born on February 6, 1954, to Percy W. Prothrow Jr. and Mildred Prothrow. The family moved to Atlanta, Georgia, when her father was named manager of Atlanta Life Insurance Company. She and her older sister attended public schools in Atlanta.

Prothrow-Stith finished high school in Houston, Texas, however. She graduated with honors from Jack Yates High School. She liked math and chose to major in it when she enrolled in Spelman College in Atlanta. Later, she shifted her major to pre-medicine and graduated magna cum laude in 1975.

Prothrow-Stith enrolled in the Harvard University Medical School, receiving her M.D. in 1979. That summer, she began serving an internship in internal medicine at Boston City Hospital, where she was shocked to see a constant stream of young victims of shootings,

stabbings, and beatings. Many of the patients died, while others were stitched up and sent back to the streets, often to return with yet another wound.

"I could not understand the blindness of my profession," Prothrow-Stith said. "How could doctors ignore a problem that killed and maimed so many young, healthy patients? . . . Could it be that no one really cared about the pointless deaths each year of thousands of young men, most of them poor, half of them black? Well, I cared."[1] While still a senior at Harvard, Prothrow-Stith began developing a way to teach young people how to constructively channel their anger.

In 1987, then thirty-three-year-old Prothrow-Stith was named Commissioner of Public Health for the state of Massachusetts, making her the first woman and the youngest person ever appointed to that position. As the person in charge of the state's health policies, she oversaw a budget of more than $300 million and a department with over 4,500 employees.

Although Prothrow-Stith held the position only two years, she was a leader in fighting tuberculosis and environmental problems. She also fought for immunizations and treatment programs for drug users and AIDS patients.

Perhaps most important of all, however, she established the nation's first violence prevention office in a state health department. Beginning in 1990, Prothrow-Stith was able to concentrate even more on finding ways to curb youth violence. In that year she was named assistant dean of government and community programs at the Harvard School of Public Health, and director of the violence program at the Harvard Injury Control Center.

Prothrow-Stith has used her positions to help develop and fund new programs, including Care for Children Hospitalized for Violent Injury, Violence Prevention Protocols for Health Care Providers, Violence Counseling Project for Students, and the Community-Based Violence Prevention Model.

She and her husband, Methodist minister Charles Stith, have two children: Percy and Mary.

One of the many honors Prothrow-Stith has received is the Rebecca Lee Award from the Massachusetts Department of Public Health (1993). Rebecca Lee, of course, was the first black woman to graduate from a medical school in the United States (see page 41).

"USE YOUR ANGER"

With the help of many people, including the confused and angry youths "eager, desperate really, for adult insight and solutions,"[2] Prothrow-Stith was able to refine her "Violence Prevention Curriculum for Adolescents" into an effective teaching tool.

Her lesson plan is now used in schools throughout the nation and in several foreign countries. The series of ten lessons ranges from providing information about violence and homicide (such as the fact that most homicides involve acquaintances or family members, not gangs) to the writing and acting out of four- or five-minute plays that are then discussed by the students.

"I have never had a student convert to non-violence right before my eyes," Prothrow-Stith wrote in her book *Deadly Consequences*, "but I do know they think about what I am saying, . . . and that is the whole point of the curriculum . . . to make them understand the control they have over their behavior and to begin to question the inevitability of fighting."[3]

All great black leaders, Prothrow-Stith points out, have had to learn how to use their anger "not to hurt oneself or one's peers, but to change the world."[4]

ELDERS, M.D.

(B .   1 9 3 3)

✦

There is probably no better measure of the progress made by black healers than the fact that two have now served as "America's family doctor"—that is, the surgeon general of the United States.

Dr. Joycelyn Elders, who was appointed to the post in 1993, was born to poor sharecroppers in Schaal, Arkansas, in 1933. She never even saw a doctor while she was growing up, much less dreamed that she could become one.

Young Joycelyn toiled in the fields alongside her parents and seven younger brothers and sisters, lived in a house without indoor plumbing, and attended racially segregated schools where her only textbooks were ones that had been used for years by white students and then discarded.

She liked studying biology and chemistry, and decided she wanted to become a laboratory technician. Officials at Philander Smith College in Little Rock, Arkansas, offered her a scholarship when she was just fifteen.

Her brothers and sisters had to join her in picking extra cotton to pay for her bus fare to Little Rock. Elders studied hard and received her B.S. degree from the college in 1952, then joined the army and became a physical therapist.

She had once been inspired by a speech by Dr. Edith lrby Jones, the first African American student to be admitted to a previously all-white southern medical school: the University of Arkansas.

Dr. Jones received her M.D. degree from the university in 1952, after enduring racial affronts throughout her years at the school.

After listening to Dr. Jones, whose philosophy about coping with prejudice and other obstacles was "to go in and be the best I can," Elders also enrolled at the University of Arkansas Medical School.[1] Despite being the only black woman and one of only three students of color in the class, Elders received her M.D. degree in 1960. She then worked as a pediatric intern at the University of Minnesota Hospital from 1960 to 1961, followed by a residency in pediatrics at the University of Arkansas Medical Center from 1961 to 1964.

During the next several years, Elders taught, maintained a private practice, and did extensive research in metabolism, growth hormones, and leukemia. She also gained recognition as an expert in the treatment of juveniles with insulin-dependent diabetes, and such patients were referred to her by doctors throughout the state.

In 1987, Elders made history when Arkansas's governor, Bill Clinton, appointed her to head the state's department of health. This marked the first time a woman or an African American had held the position. The teenage pregnancy rate in Arkansas at the time was the second highest in the nation, a fact that greatly troubled Elders. She was also concerned about the large number of out-of-wedlock births and the high rate of abortions in the state.

In an effort to combat these problems, she initiated several programs, including the distribution of condoms in schools, encouraging wider sex education for adolescents, and the establishment of school-based health clinics.

Elders wanted to discourage abortions, but she also believed in providing easier access to the procedure for those who chose it. This stand sparked furious opposition, leading the outspoken physician to respond: "Abortion foes are part of a celibate, male-dominated church, a male-dominated legislature and a male-dominated medical profession."[2]

Both her forthrightness and the controversy it engendered would follow her to Washington, D.C., where she again made history. On September 8, 1993, Elders was sworn in by President Bill Clinton as the first African American surgeon general in the history of the United States.

Her husband, Oliver—a high school basketball coach—also moved to Washington, where he became a special assistant to the intergovernmental affairs director of the U.S. Education Department. The couple have two adult children, Eric and Kevin.

"The government in the 1990s must be prepared to grapple with some very tough challenges as we focus on health care for all the people—not just the rich and privileged," she declared. ". . . We must work for a society in which people of all classes find satisfactory health care delivery a priority."[3] For the next fifteen months, Elders worked to make health care delivery a reality for all Americans.

She was often attacked for her efforts to address certain issues, however, and was forced to resign in 1994 for her opinions about teaching human sexuality.

Dr. Joycelyn Elders was proud, however, of the efforts she had made in raising awareness about vital health issues that had never been widely discussed before. "We can't solve problems if we don't talk about them," she told one interviewer.[4]

As far as the position of surgeon general was concerned, she said it had become so controversial that "Congress is ready to attack anyone who is nominated. Only God or the pope could fill the position."[5]

But Elders was wrong, and on February 10, 1998, Dr. David Satcher became the second African American surgeon general in the nation's history.

DAVID
SATCHER, M.D.

(B. 1941)

✦

"No one needs to teach him about the poor," Dr. Joycelyn Elders observed of the fifty-six-year-old Alabama native Dr. David Satcher when President Bill Clinton appointed him surgeon general in 1998.[1]

Satcher was born on May 2, 1941, on a farm a few miles outside of Anniston, Alabama, to Wilmer and Anna Satcher. Of the nine children born to his parents, one died in childbirth and another lived only a few weeks.

Though neither of his parents finished elementary school, his father taught himself to read by memorizing Bible passages he heard in church, then picking them out of the family Bible at home.

His deeply religious parents raised not only Satcher and his siblings but also the child of a relative.

"I may have come from a poor family economically, but they were not poor in spirit," Satcher once told an interviewer. "We had a rich environment from the spirit of my parents, both of whom had a vision

for their children."[2] Satcher and his siblings rose before dawn to help with the chores on their parents' 40-acre farm (his father also worked fifty-five hours every week in a foundry). Then they took the long bus ride to a rundown all-black school, passing two much more modern all-white schools on the way.

His parents were determined that their children obtain as good an education as was possible in the segregated schools available to them, and Satcher used his time on the bus to study. He soon became so good at chemistry and other subjects that he sometimes taught classes when the teachers were out sick.

After graduating from high school, Satcher enrolled in Morehouse College in Atlanta, Georgia, on a full scholarship for tuition and books.

He not only excelled academically at Morehouse, but he also became deeply involved in the civil rights movement for the first time. "My parents taught us self-respect," he remembered, "but they also adapted to the environment in which we lived. The movement in

YOU CAN MAKE YOUR DREAMS COME TRUE

Satcher's dream of becoming a doctor was born early in his life. The man who would go on to become a world leader in medicine and public health almost died of whooping cough when he was two. There was little hope for him because of the family's poverty and the refusal of white doctors to treat black patients, but the area's sole black doctor came and successfully treated the desperately ill child.

Satcher never forgot lying in the bed he shared with two brothers, coughing and barely able to breathe, then being given the medicine that helped save his life. That childhood memory, in turn, gave birth to his dream of becoming a doctor.

"I've had a mission throughout my life," he declared. "I wanted to make the greatest difference for the people who I thought had the greatest need."[3]

Atlanta was the chance to act."[4] Satcher became a member of the Student Nonviolent Coordinating Committee (SNCC) and was arrested several times for participating in sit-ins to desegregate lunch counters. Typically, the conscientious student spent his time behind bars studying.

In 1963, Satcher graduated magna cum laude from Morehouse with a B.S. degree, and was also elected to Phi Beta Kappa. He then enrolled in Case Western Reserve University, in Cleveland, Ohio, where he was one of only two African American students.

◆ **Genetics** is the scientific study of characteristics passed from one generation to the next.

Satcher studied for both an M.D. and a Ph.D. in chromosome genetics at Western Reserve, and received both degrees in 1970. He served his residency at Strong Memorial Hospital in Rochester, New York, then spent a year at a health center for migrant workers. During this period, Dr. Satcher became especially interested in sickle-cell anemia. He even made a film about it.

Sickle-cell is a hereditary disease that, in the United States, strikes primarily at people of African descent. It is also found in parts of southern Europe, Asia, and Central and South America. Approximately 1 of every 400 African Americans suffers from sickle-cell anemia.

People with sickle-cell anemia suffer from a change in their red blood cells that makes it difficult for their blood to transport oxygen to the tissues of the body. They may undergo crises during which they have severe pains in the abdomen, bones, and muscles, often accompanied by fever and signs of infection. Sickle-cell anemia has no cure, but it can be treated with antibiotics, bed rest, blood transfusions, and drugs for pain. Easing the problem of sickle-cell anemia would become a lifelong concern for young Dr. Satcher.

In 1972, Satcher left Rochester and accepted a position as director of the Community Hypertension Outreach Program at the Martin Luther King Jr. General Hospital in south-central Los Angeles. The hospital is affiliated with the Charles F. Drew Postgraduate Medical School, and Satcher joined the school as professor and chairman of the department of family medicine from 1976 to 1979.

He also found time during his seven years in Los Angeles to open a free clinic in the basement of a Baptist church in Watts and direct the King-Drew Sickle-Cell Center.

During this period, Satcher also experienced a deep loss. His first wife, Callie Frances Herndon, passed away from breast cancer in 1978. The couple had three sons and a daughter. A year and a half later, Satcher married Nola Smith, a poet.

In 1982, Satcher became president of Nashville's Meharry Medical College. At that time, Meharry trained 40 percent of the nation's African American doctors and dentists. The college, however, was on the verge of losing its accreditation when Satcher arrived, and its teaching hospital was bankrupt. Satcher managed to save both the college and the hospital. He started successful programs to combat drug abuse and other problems. Today, Meharry is a center for research on black health, turning out 15 percent of the nation's black doctors.

"If you can give young people a reason to believe that they can change the future for themselves and others," he said, "then it is much easier to deal with violence and substance abuse and teenage pregnancy. . . . We've found that those problems were not the problems, they were the symptoms [of hopelessness]."[5]

Dr. Satcher brought his commitment to helping the most vulnerable members of society to the Centers for Disease Control and Prevention, where he served as director from 1992 until his 1998 appointment as surgeon general. A Nashville official who worked with Satcher in helping to save Meharry's hospital said of him: "He was a black knight, a real effective dreamer."[6]

The same thing could be said about the generations of black healers. From Rebecca Lee moving to Virginia to help treat thousands of newly freed men, women, and children, to Charles Richard Drew probing the mysteries of human blood, to David Satcher becoming America's family doctor, African American healers have been effective dreamers.

CHRONOLOGY

1762   Dr. James Durham born

1776   Declaration of Independence signed

1812   Major Martin Robison Delany born

1813   James McCune Smith, M.D., born

1825   John S. Rock, M.D., born

        Dr. Alexander T. Augusta born

1833   Rebecca Lee (Crumpler), M.D., born

1842   Charles Burleigh Purvis, M.D., born

1845   Mary Eliza Mahoney born

1846   Rebecca Cole, M.D., born

1848   Susie King Taylor born

1856   Nathan Francis Mossell, M.D., born

        Daniel Hale Williams, M.D., born

1861   Civil War begins

1863   Fifty-fourth Massachusetts Volunteer Regiment mustered into service

        Fifty-fourth Massachusetts Volunteer Regiment assaults Fort Wagner, South Carolina

1864   George Cleveland Hall, M.D., born

1865   Civil War ends

        John S. Rock, M.D., becomes the first black American admitted to practice law before the U.S. Supreme Court

        James McCune Smith, M.D., dies

        Congress passes the Thirteenth Amendment, abolishing slavery in the United States; it is later ratified.

1866   John S. Rock, M.D., dies

1867   Congress passes the first Reconstruction Act, repairing former Confederate states to ratify the "Civil War Amendments," write new constitutions, and grant voting rights to all males, regardless of "race, color, or previous condition of servitude."

Rebecca Cole becomes the second black woman to graduate from an American medical school (Female Medical College, now Medical College of Pennsylvania)

Howard University founded in Washington, D.C.

1868 Howard University College of Medicine, founded in Washington, D.C.

Austin Maurice Curtis, M.D., born

Freedmen's Hospital founded in Washington, D.C.

1870 Adah Belle Thoms born

1871 Justina Laurena Ford, M.D., born

1876 Meharry Medical College founded in Nashville, Tennessee

1877 Reconstruction ends

1881 Tuskegee Institute founded in Tuskegee, Alabama

1883 William Augustus Hinton, M.D., born

1885 Major Martin Robison Delany dies

1890 Dr. Alexander T. Augusta dies

1891 Provident Hospital founded in Chicago

Louis Tompkins Wright, M.D., born

1893 Daniel Hale Williams, M.D., performs the first open-heart surgery

1895 Frederick Douglass Memorial Hospital and Training School for Nurses founded in Philadelphia

1896 In the case of *Plessy* v. *Ferguson*, the United States Supreme Court rules that "separate but equal" facilities for blacks are constitutional

1898 Spanish-American War

1899 Percy Lavon Julian, Ph.D., born

1902 Susie King Taylor publishes her autobiography, *Reminiscences of My Life in Camp: A Black Woman's Civil War Memoirs*

1904 Charles Richard Drew, M.D., born

1908 National Association of Colored Graduate Nurses (NACGN) founded

1909 National Association for the Advancement of Colored People founded

1912 Susie King Taylor dies

1914 World War I begins in Europe

1917	United States enters World War I
1918	World War I ends
1920	Nineteenth Amendment is ratified, giving women the right to vote
1922	Rebecca Cole, M.D., dies
1926	Mary Eliza Mahoney dies
1929	Charles Burleigh Purvis, M.D., dies
1930	George Cleveland Hall, M.D., dies
1931	Daniel Hale Williams, M.D., dies
1933	Joycelyn Jones Elders, M.D., born
1934	Alvin Francis Poussaint, M.D., born
1939	Austin Maurice Curtis, M.D., dies
	World War II begins in Europe
1941	United States enters World War II
	David Satcher, M.D., born
1942	Charles Drew, M.D., secures patent for device to preserve blood
1943	Adah Belle Thoms dies
1945	World War II ends
1946	Nathan Francis Mossell, M.D., dies
1947	National Medical Association founded
1948	Black nurses allowed to join the formerly all-white American Nurses Association
1950	Charles Richard Drew, M.D., dies
	Korean War begins
1951	National Association of Colored Graduate Nurses disbands
	Benjamin Solomon Carson, M.D., born
1952	Justina Laurena Ford, M.D., dies
	Louis Tompkins Wright, M.D., dies
1953	Korean War ends
1954	Deborah Prothrow-Stith, M.D., born
1959	William Augustus Hinton, M.D., dies

1964   Congress passes a Civil Rights Act, ending federal funding of segregated hospitals and schools

1975   Percy Lavon Julian, Ph.D., dies

1993   Joycelyn Elders, M.D., becomes the first African American surgeon general of the United States

1998   David Satcher, M.D., becomes surgeon general of the United States

NOTES

INTRODUCTION

1. "Ben Carson: Man of Miracles," *Reader's Digest* (April 1990), 74.

2. Helen Buckler, *Negro Doctor* (New York: McGraw-Hill, 1954), 83.

JAMES DURHAM

1. Herbert Morais, *The History of the Afro-American in Medicine* (Cornwells Heights, Pa.: Publishers Agency, 1976), 8.

2. Ibid., 8.

3. Winthrop D. Jordan, *White Over Black: American Attitudes Toward the Negro, 1550–1812* (Chapel Hill: University of North Carolina Press, 1968), 202.

JAMES McCUNE SMITH

1. Herbert Morais, *The History of the Afro-American in Medicine* (Cornwells Heights, Pa.: Publishers Agency, 1976), 33.

2. Ibid., 32.

3. Ibid., 33.

4. Frederick Douglass, *Life and Times of Frederick Douglass* (New York: Bonanza Books, 1962), 468.

MARTIN ROBISON DELANY

1. Rayford W. Logan, ed., *Dictionary of American Negro Biography* (New York: W.W. Norton, 1982), 172.

JOHN S. ROCK

1. Rayford W. Logan, ed., *Dictionary of American Negro Biography* (New York: W.W. Norton, 1982), 530.

2. Ibid.

3. Herbert Morais, *The History of the Afro-American in Medicine* (Cornwells Heights, Pa.: Publishers Agency, 1976), 35.

4. Logan, *Dictionary of American Negro Biography*, 530.

ALEXANDER T. AUGUSTA

1. Ira Berlin, ed., *Freedom: A Documentary History of Emancipation, 1861–1867* (New York: Cambridge University Press, 1982), 354.

2. Ibid., 355.

3. Ibid., 356.

4. Montague Cobb, *The First Negro Medical Society* (Washington, D.C.: Associated Publishers, 1939), 89.

5. Rayford W. Logan, ed., *Dictionary of American Negro Biography* (New York: W.W. Norton, 1982), 19.

SUSIE KING TAYLOR

1. Susie King Taylor, *Reminiscences of My Life in Camp: A Black Woman's Civil War Memoirs* (Princeton, N.J.: Markus Wiener Publishers, 1994), 29–30.

2. Ibid., 31.

3. Ibid., 52.

4. Ibid.

5. Thomas Wentworth Higginson, *Army Life in a Black Regiment* (New York: W.W. Norton, 1984), 89–90.

6. Taylor, *Reminiscences of My Life in Camp: A Black Woman's Civil War Memoirs*, 67.

7. Ibid., 72.

8. Ibid., 88.

9. Ibid., 124.

10. Ibid.

11. Ibid., 141.

12. Ibid., 148.

13. Ibid., 135.

14. Ibid., 151–152.

REBECCA LEE (CRUMPLER)

1. Darlene Clark Hine, ed., B*lack Women in America*, vol. 1 (Brooklyn: Carlson Publishing, 1993), 290.

2. "Outstanding Women Doctors," *Ebony* (May 1964), 68.

CHARLES BURLEIGH PURVIS

1. Rayford W. Logan, ed., *Dictionary of American Negro Biography* (New York: W.W. Norton, 1982), 508.

2. Ibid., 507.

3. Herbert Morais, *The History of the Afro-American in Medicine* (Cornwells Heights, Pa.: Publishers Agency, 1976), 52.

4. Logan, *Dictionary of American Negro Biography*, 508.

MARY ELIZA MAHONEY

1. "Mary Eliza Mahoney: The Tender Healer," *Encore American & Worldwide News* (November 27, 1978), 47.

2. Ibid.

3. Adah B. Thoms, *Pathfinders: A History of the Progress of Colored Graduate Nurses* (New York: Kay Printing House, 1929), 213–214.

4. Jessie Carney Smith, ed., *Notable Black American Women* (Detroit: Gale Research, 1992), 720.

NATHAN FRANCIS MOSSELL

1. Herbert Morais, *The History of the Afro-American in Medicine* (Cornwells Heights, Pa.: Publishers Agency, 1976), 80.

DANIEL HALE WILLIAMS

1. Herbert Morais, *The History of the Afro-American in Medicine* (Cornwells Heights, Pa.: Publishers Agency, 1976), 70.

2. "The Civil Rights Activities of Three Great Negro Physicians (1840–1940)," *Journal of Negro History* 52 (July 1967), 177.

3. Lillie Patterson, *Sure Hands, Strong Heart* (Nashville: Abingdon, 1981), 89.

4. Ibid., 96.

5. Madeline Stratton. *Negroes Who Helped Build America* (Boston: Ginn and Company, 1965), 4.

AUSTIN MAURICE CURTIS

1. Rayford W. Logan, ed., *Dictionary of American Negro Biography* (New York: W.W. Norton, 1982), 153.

ADAH BELLE THOMS

1. Herbert Morais, *The History of the Afro-American in Medicine* (Cornwells Heights, Pa.: Publishers Agency, 1976), 123–124.

2. Adah B. Thoms, *Pathfinders: A History of the Progress of Colored Graduate Nurses* (New York: Kay Printing House, 1929), 232.

3. Ibid., 162.

JUSTINA LAURENA FORD

1. Jessie Carney Smith, ed., *Notable Black American Women.* Book II (Detroit: Gale Research, 1996), 229.

2. Ibid.

3. Ibid.

4. Ibid., 230.

5. Ibid.

6. Ibid.

7. Ibid.

8. Ibid., 231.

9. Ibid.

10. Ibid., 230.

11. Ibid., 231.

LOUIS TOMPKINS WRIGHT

1. "The Civil Rights Activities of Three Great Negro Physicians (1840–1940)." *Journal of Negro History*, 52 (July 1967), 182.

2. Ibid.

3. Ibid.

4. Robert C. Hayden and Jacqueline Harris, *Nine Black American Doctors* (Reading, Mass.: Addison-Wesley, 1976), 67.

WILLIAM AUGUSTUS HINTON

1. Spencie Love, *One Blood: The Death and Resurrection of Charles R. Drew* (Chapel Hill: University of North Carolina Press, 1996), 294.

2. Robert C. Hayden, *Eleven African-American Doctors* (New York: Twenty-First Century Books, 1991), 42.

3. Herbert Morais, *The History of the Afro-American in Medicine* (Cornwells Heights, Pa.: Publishers Agency, 1976), 103.

4. Emily J. McMurray, ed., *Notable Twentieth-Century Scientists* (Detroit: Gale Research, 1995), 932.

5. Rayford W. Logan, ed., *Dictionary of American Negro Biography* (New York: W.W. Norton, 1982), 316.

6. Ibid.

7. "Dr. W. A. Hinton, 75, Of Harvard Dead," *New York Times* (August 9, 1959), 88.

8. Hayden, *Eleven African-American Doctors*, 39.

9. Logan, *Dictionary of American Negro Biography*, 316.

CHARLES RICHARD DREW

1. Spencie Love, *One Blood: The Death and Resurrection of Charles R. Drew* (Chapel Hill: University of North Carolina Press, 1996), 141–142.

2. Ibid., 121.

3. Ibid., 143.

4. Ibid., 149.

5. Madeline Stratton, *Negroes Who Helped Build America* (Boston: Ginn and Company, 1965), 19–20.

6. Robert C. Hayden, *Seven Black American Scientist*s (Reading, Mass.: Addison-Wesley, 1970), 184.

7. Love, *One Blood: The Death and Resurrection of Charles R. Drew*, 165.

8. "Charles Drew's 'Other' Medical Revolution," *Ebony* (February 1974), 88.

9. Love, *One Blood: The Death and Resurrection of Charles R. Drew,* 15.

10. "Charles Drew's 'Other' Medical Revolution," 89.

11. Ibid., 95.

PERCY LAVON JULIAN

1. Louis Haber, *Black Pioneers of Science and Invention* (New York: Harcourt Brace, 1970), 136.

2. "Percy L. Julian's Fight for His Life," *Ebony* (March 1975), 100.

3. Ibid., 94.

4. Herbert Morais, *The History of the Afro-American in Medicine* (Cornwells Heights, Pa.: Publishers Agency, 1976), 1.

5. Haber. *Black Pioneers of Science and Invention*, 144.

ALVIN FRANCIS POUSSAINT

1. "'Cosby Show' Adviser Brings Parenting Tips to Workshops," *Knight-Ridder News Service* (March 22, 1994), 2.

2. Ibid., 3.

3. Herbert Morais, *The History of the Afro-American in Medicin*e (Cornwells Heights, Pa.: Publishers Agency, 1976), 188.

4. Ibid., 173.

5. Charles Moritz, ed., *Current Biography* (New York: H. W. Wilson, 1973), 334.

6. Ibid., 335.

7. "'Cosby Show' Adviser Brings Parenting Tips to Workshops," 2.

BENJAMIN SOLOMON CARSON

1. "Surgical Superstar," *Ebony* (January 1988), 56.

2. Ibid.

3. "Ben Carson: Man of Miracles," *Reader's Digest* (April 1990), 75.

DEBORAH PROTHROW-STITH

1. Deborah Prothrow-Stith, *Deadly Consequences: How Violence Is Destroying Our Teenage Population and a Plan to Begin Solving the Problem* (New York: Harper-Collins, 1991), 3.

2. Ibid., 134.

3. Ibid., 179–180.

4. Ibid., 183.

JOYCELYN JONES ELDERS

1. Jessie Carney Smith, ed., *Notable Black American Women.* Book II (Detroit: Gale Research, 1992), 347.

2. Ibid., 201.

3. Ibid.

4. "Senate Confirms Satcher," Associated Press Story, *Daily Gazette* (Schenectady, N.Y., February 11, 1998), A1.

5. Ibid.

DAVID SATCHER

1. "Senate Confirms Satcher," Associated Press Story, *Daily Gazette* (Schenectady, N.Y., February 11, 1998), A1.

2. Elizabeth A. Schick, ed., *Current Biography* 58, no. 9 (February 1997), 487.

3. Ibid.

4. Ibid.

5. Ibid., 489.

6. "America's Doctor," *New York Times* (September 13, 1997), A8.

BIBLIOGRAPHY

BOOKS

Haber, Louis. *Black Pioneers of Science and Invention.* New York: Harcourt, Brace & Co., 1992.

Hayden, Robert C. *Eleven African American Doctors.* Frederick, Md.: Twenty-First Century Books, a division of Henry Holt & Co., 1992.

———. *Seven Black American Scientists.* Reading, Mass.: Addison-Wesley, 1970.

Hine, Darlene Clark, ed. *Black Women in America: An Historical Encyclopedia.* Brooklyn: Carlson Publishing Inc., 1993.

Kaufman, Martin, Stuart Galishoff, and Todd L. Savitt, eds. *Dictionary of American Medical Biography.* Westport, Conn.: Greenwood Press, 1984.

Kaye, Judith. *The Life of Daniel Hale Williams.* New York: Twenty-First Century Books, a division of Henry Holt & Co., 1993.

Love, Spencie. *One Blood: The Death and Resurrection of Charles R. Drew.* Chapel Hill: University of North Carolina Press, 1996.

McMurray, Emily J. *Notable Twentieth-Century Scientists.* Detroit: Gale Research Inc., 1995.

Morais, Herbert M. *The History of the Afro-American in Medicine.* Cornwells Heights, Pa.: Publishers Agency, under the auspices of the Association for the Study of Afro-American Life and History, 1976.

Patterson, Lillie. *Sure Hands, Strong Heart: The Life of Daniel Hale Williams.* Nashville: Abingdon, 1981.

Prothrow-Stith, Deborah. *Deadly Consequences: How Violence Is Destroying Our Teenage Population and a Plan to Begin Solving the Problem.* New York: Harper-Collins, 1991.

Robinson, Wilhelmina S. *Historical Afro-American Biographies.* Cornwells Heights, Pa.: Publishers Agency, under the auspices of the Association for the Study of Afro-American Life and History, 1976.

Sammons, Vivian Ovelton. *Blacks in Science and Medicine.* New York: Hemisphere Publishing Corp., 1990.

Schick, Elizabeth A. *Current Biography.* New York: H.W. Wilson Co., 1997.

Smith, Jessie Carney, ed. *Notable Black American Women.* Detroit: Gale Research Inc., 1997.

Staupers, Mabel Keaton. *No Time for Prejudice: A Story of the Integration of Negroes in Nursing in the United States.* New York: Macmillan, 1961.

PERIODICALS

Anonymous. "Second Class Medicine." *Encore American & Worldwide News* (November 27, 1978): 48–53.

Anonymous. "Mary Eliza Mahoney: The Tender Healer." *Encore American & Worldwide News* (November 27, 1978): 47.

Bims, Hamilton. "Percy L. Julian's Fight for His Life." *Ebony* (March 1975): 94–104.

————. "Charles Drew's 'Other' Medical Revolution." *Ebony* (February 1974): 88–96.

Cobb, W. Montague. "Louis Tompkins Wright, 1891–1952." *Journal of the National Medical Association* (March 1953): 130–148.

————. "A Short History of Freedmen's Hospital." *Journal of the National Medical Association* 54, no. 3 (May 1962): 271–287.

Drew, Charles Richard. "Negro Scholars in Scientific Research." *Journal of Negro History* 35 (April 1950): 135–149.

Link, Eugene P. "The Civil Rights Activities of Three Great Negro Physicians." *Journal of Negro History* 52 (July, 1967): 169–184.

Miller, Kelly. "The Historic Background of the Negro Physician." *Journal of Negro History* 1 (April 1916): 99–109.

Phillips, Christopher. "Ben Carson: Man of Miracles." *Reader's Digest* (April 1990): 71–75.

Worthy, Dr. William. "An Appreciation of Dr. Hinton" (letter). *New England Journal of Medicine* (September 18, 1952): 453.

Wright, Louis T. "Factors Controlling Negro Health." *The Crisis* 42, no. 9 (September 1935): 264–265, 280–281, 284.

NEWSPAPERS

Anonymous. "Harvard Names First Negro Professor." *New York Times* (June 30, 1949): 48.

Anonymous. "Dr. Louis Wright, Noted Physician, 61" (obituary). *New York Times* (October 9, 1952): 31.

Brody, Jane E. "Twin Boys Are Separated in 22 Hours of Surgery." *New York Times* (September 7, 1987): 1, 8.

PICTURE CREDITS

Pages 6 and 11: courtesy of the Library of Congress, Washington, D.C.; page 12: public domain; page 18: courtesy of Art Resource, National Portrait Gallery/Smithsonian Institution, Washington, D.C.; page 22: courtesy of Freedmen's Bureau, Library of Congress, Washington, D.C.; pages 24 and 29: courtesy of Library of Congress, Washington, D.C.; page 35: courtesy of Moorland-Spingarn Research Center, Howard University, Washington, D.C.; page 38: courtesy of National Archives; page 42: public domain; page 43: courtesy of Photographs and Print Division, Schomburg Center for Research in Black Culture, The New York Public Library/Astor, Lenox and Tilden Foundations; page 47: courtesy of Medical Department, Howard University, Washington, D.C.; page 54: courtesy of Moorland-Spingarn Research Center, Howard University, Washington, D.C.; page 57: courtesy of Hampton University (Va.) Archives; pages 59 and 64: courtesy of the Library of Congress, Washington, D.C.; page 68: courtesy of Moorland-Spingarn Research Center, Howard University, Washington, D.C.; page 71: courtesy of the Library of Congress, Washington, D.C.; page 74: Moorland-Spingarn Research Center, Howard University, Washington, D.C.; page 77: courtesy of Photographs and Print Division, Schomburg Center for Research in Black Culture, The New York Public Library/Astor, Lenox and Tilden Foundations; page 82: courtesy of the Black American West Museum and Heritage Center, Denver; page 85: courtesy of the Colorado Historical Society, Denver; page 88: courtesy of Photographs and Print Division, Schomburg Center for Research in Black Culture, The New York Public Library/Astor, Lenox and Tilden Foundations; page 92: courtesy of the Library of Congress, Washington, D.C.; page 93: courtesy of New York Medical College; page 95: courtesy of Harvard University Medical School, Cambridge, Mass.; page 101: courtesy of the American

INDEX

Page numbers in **boldface** indicate subjects of articles.

New York Manumission Society, 10
Nineteenth Amendment, 55–56
North Star (newspaper), 13, 19
Northwestern University Medical
    School, 63, 73
nurses
    black professional organization,
        55, 56, 78
    Civil War, 1, 34, 37, 38–39
    education, 53, 65, 66, 76, 78
    first black graduate, 53
    public health, 78, 79
    World War I, 79, 80
Nursing Hall of Fame, 57

Oberlin College, 48
obstetrics, 83
    defined, 89
104th U.S. Colored Troops, 21
Onesimus, 8
outpatients, defined, 61

Palmer, Dr. Henry, 63
pathology, 119
Payne, Daniel, 28
pediatrics
    defined, 96
    neurosurgery, 123, 125–27
Penn, Dr. William Fletcher, 87
pericardium suture, 66, 67
Peter Stuyvesant High School
    (N.Y.C.), 117
pharmacy, 12
Philadelphia, 44, 91
    African American hospital, 60–61
    diphtheria epidemic, 5, 7–8
Philander Smith College, 132, 133

physostigmine, 111–12
Pittsburgh, 19–20
plasma. *See* blood plasma
Poussaint, Alvin Francis, M.D.,
    117–22
practice, defined, 12
Principia of Ethnology (Delany),
    21–22
Proctor Prize, 114
progesterone, 113
Prothrow-Stith, Deborah, M.D.,
    128–31
Provident Hospital (Chicago),
    66–67, 70, 73, 75, 80
    new building, 72
psychiatry, 120, 121–22
    defined, 96
psychology, defined, 96
public health, 44, 78–79, 98
Public Health Department, Massa-
    chusetts, 96, 130
Public Health Service, U.S., 93, 98
Pullman, George, 65
Purvis, Charles Burleigh, M.D.,
    46–50
Purvis, Robert Sr., 48

racial discrimination, 26, 39
    hospital staff practice, 65, 83, 89,
        103
    medical societies, 32, 50, 83, 119
    nurse education, 53, 65, 78
    nursing practice, 55, 60, 61–62
    obstetrics practice, 89
    post–World War II to mid-1960s,
        119
    psychological effects of, 120, 121